Britain's Rail Routes Past and Present

THE EAST COAST MAIN LINE

King's Cross to Newcastle: the route of the 'Silver Jubilee'

HOLLOWAY BANK: Nothing changes? *Silver Link*'s sister loco, Class 'A4' 'Pacific' No 60015 *Quicksilver*, powers up Holloway Bank on 11 May 1953 with a relief express from King's Cross to Glasgow via Edinburgh Waverley. The stock mixture, arrived at by coupling together whatever the control office could lay its hands on, is typical of relief services of that period, but the locomotive looks in fine fettle.

At the same position on 29 October 1994 another 'A4', No 60009 *Union of South Africa*, hauls a special *Steam Railway* magazine charter train from King's Cross to Peterborough carrying 'The Elizabethan' headboard. It is just 30 years after the same engine left the London terminus with the 'final' steam working! The photograph is reproduced by kind permission of EMAP, publishers of *Steam Railway*. *Both BM*

Britain's Rail Routes Past and Present

THE EAST COAST MAIN LINE

King's Cross to Newcastle: the route of the 'Silver Jubilee'

Geoffrey Body

Principal photographer Brian Morrison

Foreword by Brian Burdsall

Managing Director, InterCity East Coast Ltd

Silver Link Publishing Ltd

First published in September 1995

British Library Cataloguing in Publication Data

A catalogue record for this book is available from the British Library.

ISBN 1 85794 052 0

Silver Link Publishing Ltd
Unit 5
Home Farm Close
Church Street
Wadenhoe
Peterborough PE8 5TE
Tel/fax (01832) 720440

Printed and bound in Great Britain

Key to Map/Diagrams

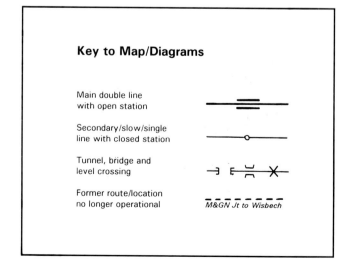

Main double line with open station	
Secondary/slow/single line with closed station	
Tunnel, bridge and level crossing	
Former route/location no longer operational	M&GN Jt to Wisbech

CONTENTS

Foreword by Brian Burdsall,
Managing Director,
InterCity East Coast Ltd   6

Introduction   7

A history of the East Coast Main Line   9

1 **'The Cross'**   18
King's Cross and Belle Isle   19
Holloway Bank   29
Finsbury Park and Harringay   37

2 **North through Wood Green**   42
Ferme Park and Hornsey   43
Wood Green and Palace Gates   46
Oakleigh Park and New Barnet   52

3 **Hatfield and Welwyn**   58
Hadley Wood and Potters Bar   59
Welham Green and Hatfield   66
Welwyn   70

4 **Hertfordshire into Bedfordshire**   76
Knebworth and Stevenage   77
Hitchin to Offord   81

5 **Huntingdon and Peterborough**   88
Huntingdon area   89
Peterborough   94
North to Essendine   100

6 **Grantham and Newark**   104
Stoke Bank   105
Grantham   108
Newark   111

7 **Trent to Don**   114
North of Newark   115
Retford   119

8 **Doncaster**   122
Southern approaches   123
Doncaster station   127
Doncaster Works   132

9 **Selby and York**   134
Selby   135
York   141

10 **Thirsk and Northallerton**   152
Pilmoor and Thirsk   153
Northallerton to Croft Spa   159

11 **Darlington and Durham**   162
Darlington   163
Durham   169

12 **Chester-le-Street and Newcastle**   172
Chester-le-Street and Tyne Yard   173
Gateshead   177
Newcastle-upon-Tyne   180

Appendix: table of distances   191
Index   192

FOREWORD

by
Brian Burdsall
Managing Director, InterCity East Coast Ltd

When I came to East Coast in 1992 as Route Director, I knew two things. Firstly, I had joined one of the best passenger railway operations in Britain, if not the world. Secondly, InterCity East Coast has a history and tradition behind it that most employees are aware of and seek to live up to.

The East Coast tradition and reputation precede the 'Silver Jubilee' train, of course. I suppose that it starts back at about the time of the Stirling 'Singles'. However, today most people have a mental picture of Gresley 'Pacifics' as the zenith of steam locomotive development, and of the late '30s streamlined trains as a high point of technical and passenger service development of the pre-war railway.

There are people even today who see this era as the high point of the London to Scotland railway, and that it has all been downhill since. Not surprisingly, I disagree with this view. A cursory glance at old timetables shows that the pre-war train service was slow and infrequent by today's standards.

This is not to denigrate the achievements of my predecessors. The important point is to view them within the context of the technical and market situation of their own period. The limiting factors for the timetable of 60 years ago were the amount of tractive effort that an 'A4' locomotive could produce, very restrictive track layouts, and a society with a much lower personal disposable income and predisposition to travel than now.

The important thing is that each generation of East Coast railway people has given their best shot to maximising the benefits that they offer the passenger - and to running a commercial business. In the context of the lead times that railway investment requires, this has involved taking the long view. It is also much more than just buying faster trains and rewriting the timetable. Each step forward in locomotives has required as much or more upgrading of track and signalling. As important as speed is the comfort of the coaches and the levels of personal service offered to the passenger. The 'Silver Jubilee' must have been a step change in both fields.

In the competitive '90s we take the need to create 'unique selling points' for granted. Sixty years ago, when rail had few competitors, it must have been a bold decision to build a small fleet of specialised rolling-stock and provide such a high level of on-board service. It would have been so easy to be complacent. I wonder how much the decision was influenced by company pride in addition to the Commercial Manager's desire for more revenue!

We can see now that the 1930s were the end of an era in both technology and social environment. Today change has become a way of life in business. East Coast services are on the brink of being run again by a private company for the first time in nearly 50 years. I do not know who will be running the privatised East Coast rail franchise, but I am sure that the commercial and service ethics that gave the route the 'Silver Jubilee' 60 years ago will be as strong in the future. My successor decades from now will still be able to start the Foreword to a book such as this with my first paragraph.

INTRODUCTION

I was very young at the time the London & North Eastern Railway introduced the 'Silver Jubilee' services, but my memory retains the excitement of the occasion, if not the detail. It must have had something in common with the opening of early railways, for the concept of streamlining was still a vague, 'foreign' fad and had not achieved any real substance in Great Britain, giving the 1935 event a novelty that only 'firsts' can command. I distinctly remember the atmosphere of mystery that existed beforehand, building up the general expectation that 'something' was going to happen, but only a privileged few knew what.

I'm really not sure just how much Dad knew. He was an LNER relief clerk at the time, one of a fairly select group prepared to go anywhere - Arlesey to Arksey, was his proud boast - and do anything, and famed for its part in the grapevine process of gathering and disseminating unofficial news. The relief clerks based at the modest ex-GNR brick building outside Peterborough North station were no exception to the search for inside knowledge, and were certainly well aware of the date and time on which the first services were to be expected.

Along with quite a host of other members of the large Peterborough railway community we were at the station in good time for the first down service. The expectations were high, but when the train came - at modest speed because of the low speed restriction through the old station - there was none of the cheering of an opening day, just a communal buzz of excitement, awe and approval. The locomotive was a new shape, the stock a new design, the livery a new colour. Here was something bold and enterprising and our company had achieved it!

Ten years and a World War were to pass by before I joined the LNER as a 'temporary probationary junior male clerk', but I suspect the event had an inevitability about it that was not unconnected with the 'Silver Jubilee' and the streamlined era it ushered in. When I did start it was to be at a station on the East Coast Main Line, and the excitement of the route from King's Cross to the North was confirmed in my blood. It had a status that lesser routes could not enjoy, even in such periods as that of the 'Britannias' on the Great Eastern main line to Norwich. In the days of the Eastern Region Line Managers, John Willie Dedman might boast about the profitability of the LT&S and the colourful Willie Thorpe about Great Eastern electrification or his new yard at Temple Mills, but Gerry Fiennes's East Coast people remained infuriatingly superior.

There was a down side, of course. Anyone catching the 4.10 pm 'Mark Lane' from King's Cross to somewhere like Sandy, or the 5.50 pm Peterborough/Cambridge service that followed, could expect to spend a significant amount of the journey on the Slow line or waiting at a turnout while the evening expresses thundered majestically past. In those days the curves had not been ironed out and the bottlenecks remained, compelling expresses, 'parleys', fitted express freights and many lesser workings to compete for a finite number of paths. Delays, derailments, hot boxes and other incidents were all fairly frequent occurrences, there to be triumphed over, and many a winter coach had as much ice inside the windows as outside when steam heating pipes got frozen up. Mercifully, today's passengers know little about such things.

Just thinking about the East Coast Main Line brings a host of memories flooding back, like the heady thrill of crossing the Tyne, imposing Durham followed by the flat crossing of the pioneer S&D at Darlington, then the lively runs across the Vale of York to the busy, curved magnificence of York station. I remember Gateshead and March drivers changing over at Doncaster and having serious communication problems because of their strong dialects, and also hurtling south in the brake of a Class C fish train, a decidedly bruising but exhilarating experience.

Grantham shed always offered interest and variety and was a prelude to Stoke Bank, where one always hoped something dramatic would happen. At the foot of the bank Essendine's unique branches were quite unforgettable and presaged the clutter of New England, the Nene crossing at Peterborough and the brickyards beyond. Market garden country then gave way to the land of the 'N2s' and 'quad art' sets before the final struggle into King's Cross via a, sometimes prolonged, view of the Star Brush Works.

When the first electrification money went to the West Coast route the main line out of King's Cross seemed rejected for a period, but then shook itself out of depression with the aid of the admirable 'Deltics'. Slowly the upper speed limits rose as the old shackles imposed by the Offord curves, Peterborough station and a dozen other constraints were removed, and timings, performance and passenger carryings responded to these stimuli. The InterCity 125 High Speed

Trains maintained this momentum, as, in its own way, did the Selby Diversion. Speed records began to tumble until the stage was set for electrification and today's excellence, which so much carries on the tradition started by the 'Silver Jubilee' services back in 1935.

As the first of a new breed of locomotive, not only streamlined in outline but with a higher performance deriving from the internal streamlining of steam passages and other improvements, *Silver Link* is inextricably associated with the 'Silver Jubilee' events. It has its high place in the annals of the East Coast Main Line not only because it worked the 'Silver Jubilee' services unaided for the first two weeks until *Silver Fox*, *Silver King* and *Quicksilver* were ready, but also by virtue of its own intrinsic engineering excellence.

Silver Link Publishing shares a significant, if lesser, anniversary with its illustrious locomotive namesake, and the writer has been privileged with an insight into the firm's recent, formative years. In terms of hard striving for excellence, the two Silver Link's have much in common.

This 1973 view of Peterborough station after reconstruction captures the essence of the changes to the East Coast Main Line. The new down platform is on the left, with the through lines in the centre and the modified former up platform on the right. *BR*

A HISTORY OF THE
EAST COAST MAIN LINE

The very first section of the East Coast Main Line started life as part of the Stockton & Darlington Railway's Croft branch, which opened in 1829. Ten years later it was purchased by the Great North of England Railway for £20,000 and the northern section, from Darlington Bank Top to Parkgate Junction, was used to form part of the projected railway northwards from Darlington towards the Tyne. However, in 1839 completion of this section was still five years and several alterations away, while that of a through East Coast route to Scotland would have to wait until the middle of the century.

The first effective rail services from London to Edinburgh via the East Coast route became possible once the permanent bridge across the Tweed had opened for passenger traffic on 29 August 1850 and a billed 'through connection' was being offered from London by the following month. But the journey was an undertaking that the modern rail traveller would have found extraordinarily complicated and exhausting. Although the Great Northern Railway's line from Maiden Lane in London to Werrington near Peterborough had been open since 7 August and had replaced the previous Eastern Counties Railway route from Shoreditch via Cambridge and Ely, the working on the new main line had not really had time to settle down and confusion was still much in evidence.

North of Werrington, work on the 'Towns Line' through Grantham was making progress, but for another two years the long-distance traveller would have to go round via Boston and Lincoln to rejoin the main route at Retford. Then, from Doncaster on to York, the journey was via the Lancashire & Yorkshire Railway to Knottingley, then over the York & North Midland Railway through Burton Salmon and Milford. From the new station at York, opened nearly three months earlier, passenger services northwards had begun on 30 March 1841, the trains of the Great North of England Railway following today's straight, fast route as far as Darlington. North of that point the original aspirations of the GNofE had passed to the Newcastle & Darlington Junction Railway, which had cobbled together a link to the Tyne from 19 June 1844. From Parkgate Junction it ran to Ferryhill, then via Shincliffe, Rainton Crossing, Washington and Pelaw to approach Gateshead from the east over the pioneer Brandling Junction company's line. A cut-off via Usworth shortened the Washington-Pelaw stretch from September 1849, passenger trains using it from 1 October 1850.

Trains were able to cross the Tyne by means of a temporary bridge from 29 August 1848 to continue over the Newcastle & Berwick Railway's 1847 line as far as Tweedmouth. From 10 October 1848 a temporary version of the eventual Royal Border Bridge began to take over from the ferry services across the Tweed and permit a rail connection with the North British company's line, which had reached the border from Edinburgh on 22 June 1846. The Tyne and Tweed crossings became permanent from 1849 and 1850 respectively.

The first major change to this meandering route took place when the 'Towns Line' between Werrington and Retford was brought into use for passengers on 1 August 1852. With the Great Northern Railway then able to get to York in five hours, the Scottish capital was brought within 11 of London, a whole hour better than the rival Euston route could achieve. By 1860 there was a regular through train leaving King's Cross between 9 and 9.30 am with stock owned jointly by the three participating railways (the Great

Northern, the North Eastern, which had been formed in 1854, and the North British). Under the impetus of an 1862 International Exhibition in London and of the North British Railway's expansion north and west from Edinburgh, this became the 'Special Scotch Express' from June 1862, and thus gave birth to the legendary 'Flying Scotsman' service. Departing at 10 am, dropping a Manchester/Sheffield portion at Retford and spending 20 minutes at York while passengers consumed a hurried meal in the refreshment rooms, the train took 10½ hours to get to Edinburgh, a significant achievement but over six hours longer than the present-day service.

The next decade brought two more major changes to the main line, the first replacing the original L&Y/NMR route to York with a link from Shaftholme Junction to Selby and another on from Barlby to Chaloner Whin Junction, 2 miles south of York. This more direct line was brought into use on 2 January 1871 and was followed on 15 January 1872 by a new route between Parkgate Junction, Darlington and Gateshead. The latter was achieved by building a new NER line between Tursdale and Relly Mill junctions to connect at the latter with the 1857 N&DJ Bishop Auckland-Leamside branch, then on via the 1868 Team Valley route from Newton Hall Junction to Gateshead.

Following the completion of agreements

between the Great Northern, North Eastern and North British companies in 1854, the line from King's Cross to Scotland began to be seen as an entity. By 1860 there were plans for joint stock and through express services leading to regular liaison meetings and eventual speed improvements. The initial 10½-hour schedule improved to 9, including the York lunch stop, then came down to 8½ after the 1888 'Race to Edinburgh' had shown what was possible. The introduction of dining cars from 1900 and opening of King Edward Bridge, Newcastle, in 1906 contributed further slight improvements in the best King's Cross-Edinburgh times, but these generally remained at 8¼ hours or more as heavier loads consumed the dividends produced by larger engines, and neither East nor West Coast managements seemed keen to break the truce that had followed the earlier racing.

Motive power on the developing East Coast route was left to the Great Northern and North Eastern companies, the former using 2-2-2 and 4-2-2 'singles' on the section to York, and the latter continuing the journey with 2-4-0s and 4-4-0s.

Between King's Cross and Newcastle the East Coast Main Line used to serve over 25 major junctions, each of which fed in traffic to the trunk route. One of the more rural examples was Essendine, pictured on 11 September 1958 with Class 'N5' 0-6-2T No 69293 about to take over the Stamford branch working from 'C12' 4-4-2T No 67398. *Philip H. Wells*

Through trains changed engines at Grantham and Newcastle as well as at York. In due course Sturrock and Fletcher engines gave way to those of Patrick Stirling, and the NER Worsdells and 'singles' to the use of 4-4-0s throughout. The delightful Ivatt 4-4-0s were replaced by his 'Atlantics' in the south, then the arrival of the Gresley-modified large 'Atlantics' and of Raven's NER 4-6-0s carried the ECML top trains through to the LNER era and confirmed the route's reputation for speed and reliability. Especially impressive was the fact that the GN fast passenger trains out of King's Cross around 1920 got no pilot assistance unless the load exceeded 66 axles!

Before the Great Northern bowed out it introduced the first of Gresley's 'Pacific' engines in the shape of numbers 1470 and 1471, the latter averaging 51.88 mph on a non-stop King's Cross to Grantham run on 3 September 1922. More of these engines allowed the LNER to introduce the 'Harrogate Pullman' and usher in the true express era, the 'Flying Scotsman' getting a new train in 1924, the set including Gresley's new articulated

dining cars with electric cooking. The 1925 exchange trials with the GWR then pointed the way for improvements in the design of the Gresley 'Pacifics', which would ease coal and water requirements and increase the scope for non-stop running. Long-travel valves successfully cut coal consumption, with more dividends following when larger boilers were fitted, permitting a pressure rise from 180 to 220 psi. In July 1927 No 1480N/4480 *Enterprise* became the first 'A1' to be so fitted, reclassified 'A3'. In the same month non-stop services began between King's Cross and Newcastle, and non-stop running over the whole East Coast route between King's Cross and Edinburgh now became a realistic objective.

The big obstacle was crewing, but this problem was solved by more Gresley innovation in the shape of the corridor tender, which allowed a crew changeover *en route* without having to stop the train. Two of these heavy tenders were available in time for an inaugural run on 1 May 1928 when No 4472 *Flying Scotsman* took the down train to Edinburgh in 8 hours 2 minutes, although No 2580 *Shotover* needed 12 minutes more for the up journey. By the end of the season the 368-ton, 11-coach train, with its cocktail bar, ladies' retiring room, hairdressing saloon and travelling W. H.

A typical steam shed scene: West Hartlepool (51C)-allocated 'A8' Class 'Pacific' tank No 69871 is attended to at Gateshead shed on 26 August 1954 while 'A3' 'Pacific' No 60036 *Colombo* awaits its turn at the water column. *BM*

Smith newsman, was to carry nearly 40,000 passengers.

The modifications to Gresley's big engines culminated in the appearance of the first purpose-built 'A3' super-'Pacific' (No 2743 *Felstead*) in August 1928 and set the stage for a new period of express passenger train achievement. With engines of this calibre and so much power to spare, the agreement between West and East Coast routes to maintain traditional timings came under increasing pressure. By mutual consent between the LMS and LNER it ended in 1932 and was marked by a cut to 7 hours 50 minutes in the journey time of the 'Flying Scotsman' in May, with a further 20-minute cut in the summer. Lesser trains followed suit, the 'Scarborough Flyer' getting a 15-minute cut in 1933 by running non-stop as far as York.

In 1934, as No 2001 *Cock of the North* appeared to herald 2-8-2 power for the services north of Edinburgh, new speed records were being established in Germany and the United States, and Great Britain had to no intention of being eclipsed. Gresley took a trip on Germany's streamlined 'Fliegende Hamburger' in 1934, and the LNER followed this with a light train test between London and Leeds in the November, preferring to match its tried and tested steam power with a light train rather than adopt the diesel option. Soon rumours of something big began to circulate, fuelled by a London-Newcastle trial run on 5 March 1935 with super-'A3' No 2750 *Papyrus* and a six-coach train. On the up working *Papyrus* ran at over 100 mph between Corby and Tallington, and set a new record with a top speed of 108 mph near Little Bytham.

Then on 27 September came the press launch of Britain's first streamlined train, the 'Silver Jubilee'. Behind *Silver Link*, the first of the 'A4' 'Pacifics', the 230-ton trial train ran at over 100 mph all the way from Hatfield to Huntingdon, and set up a new 112½ mph record on the flat stretch north of Hitchin. With valances added to streamline the articulated seven-coach set, which was luxuriously furnished inside and finished in a silver-grey alloy outside, the new train made an impressive sight with its locomotive also streamlined inside and out to give a good aerodynamic shape and free steaming. The public service began on 30 September with a 4-hour up journey leaving Newcastle at 10 am and returning at 5.30 pm, both with a stop at Darlington. *Silver Link* was soon joined at King's Cross by *Silver Fox* and *Quicksilver*, and by *Silver King* as spare engine at Gateshead.

So successful was the new service that the LNER was soon thinking of a similar facility for Edinburgh, and ordering more 'A4s' to facilitate this. Among the preparations was a test run on 27 August 1936 when, with a dynamometer car added to the 'Silver Jubilee' set, No 2512 *Silver Fox* established a new record in the up direction with a speed of 113 mph at milepost 86. On 29 June of the following year the LMS claimed 114 mph for a precipitate arrival at Crewe, and the LNER response with a trial run of its new 'Coronation' service on the following day could only manage 109½ mph on the return from Barkston.

However, the new 'Coronation' public service, which began on 5 July 1937, was an immediate success. Two new articulated and streamlined sets were provided, painted in light Marlborough Blue and the darker Garter Blue, and with the last vehicle of the nine an observation saloon. Leaving King's Cross at 4 pm and Edinburgh at 4.30 pm, the 6-hour journey was entrusted to a new build of 'A4s', *Union of South Africa*, *Dominion of Canada*, *Commonwealth of Australia*, *Empire of India* and *Dominion of New Zealand*. Two more such engines, *Golden Fleece* and *Golden Shuttle*, and a third 'Coronation' set, were allocated to the 'West Riding Limited' when it joined the streamlined services from 27 September with a booking of 185 minutes for its 195-mile run to Leeds/Bradford. Operated with two clear block sections ahead to reduce the risk of delays and allow ample stopping distance, the new services achieved an excellent record of punctuality.

On the continent the German State Railways pushed the world speed record up to 125 mph, while at home braking trials were occupying much attention, since brake capacity was now the main factor inhibiting speed. On 3 July 1938 No 4468 *Mallard* was booked for one such trial with a load of 'Coronation' vehicles plus dynamometer car. Sir Nigel Gresley himself was on the test train together with a number of Westinghouse employees, the latter being given the option of leaving the train before the return journey, which was to be a high-speed run. After turning via the Barkston triangle *Mallard* took it easy through the 24 mph permanent way restriction at Grantham, then lifted its 273-ton train rapidly to Stoke Summit, where the speed reached 70 mph. On down Stoke Bank the readings climbed rapidly to 125 mph approaching milepost 91, and to a fraction over 126 mph a mile further on. For an exhilarating 5 miles the speed had averaged 120.4 mph, and the world record for steam was back in LNER hands.

The two steam locomotive designs that dominated express running on the East Coast Main Line in the pre-war years: Gresley's 'A4' 'Pacific' No 4498 *Sir Nigel Gresley* and 'A3' Class No 4472 *Flying Scotsman*, both happily preserved, are pictured at the Rocket 150 celebrations in 1980. *British Rail*

In September 1939 the streamliners were withdrawn as a prelude to the long wartime years of strife and austerity. During those years the LNER carried massive quantities of freight and strategic materials, its passengers managing with a scaled-down public service that at busy times was packed to near impossible levels. The system absorbed its share of air raid punishment, including a direct hit on the King's Cross main office block at the height of the blitz and later rocket damage to the track between Hornsey and Wood Green. The East Coast Main Line played a significant part in the transportation of war materials and personnel, as did the Gresley locomotives, from the suddenly unkempt 'A4s' to the delightful all-purpose 'V2s', the hard-working 'K3s' and the many lesser types.

The LNER emerged from the war grimy and worn but with a determination to rebuild. By 1946 it had published *Forward*, a £90 million plan for rejuvenating the system, including many improvements along the East Coast Main Line, some later to be achieved and others - like the proposed new marshalling yard at Oakleigh Park - quietly forgotten. The 'A2' 'Pacifics' appeared in 1946 and *Silver Fox* performed creditably on a track test special, reaching Edinburgh in 378½ minutes and achieving the magic 100 mph figure on the return journey.

The last year of the LNER was marked by coal shortages, a nasty accident at Doncaster and a terrible winter. Then on 12 August 1948 extensive flooding breached the East Coast Main Line north of Berwick and affected the newly restored non-stop summer 'Flying Scotsman' service, but the winter produced a 'Tees-Tyne Pullman', and more named services appeared in 1949. Actress Anne Crawford launched the King's Cross-Edinburgh non-stop 'Capitals Limited' on 23 May, with the 'Northumbrian', 'The White Rose' and 'The West Riding' beginning in the summer; the latter used surviving 'Coronation' vehicles.

The 1950s began with a farewell to the last Ivatt 'Atlantic', No 62822, which worked a special to Doncaster on 26 November as a final grand gesture before being scrapped. The 4-6-2s were then regrouped, with provision for most of the express services to change engines at Grantham.

Despite the LNER's grand plans the infrastructure of the ECML remained little changed with the exception of a few wartime extras like the Up and Down Slow between Thirsk and Pilmoor and the slow post-war recovery of the arrears of maintenance. Express services still had to contest the bottlenecks at Hadley Wood, Welwyn, Arlesey and Sandy with suburban and freight workings, and to slow for the curves through Offord and Peterborough and through York and Durham. Then, at last, 1952 brought the first signs of real change with British Transport Commission approval for the first Potters Bar scheme, this providing for a new station with up and down islands and with two extra tracks south to the first of the tunnels.

Commissioning of the new Potters Bar station in 1955 was some compensation for the ASLEF train crew strike that began on Whit Saturday. This was also a period of freight rationalisation, with a series of reclassifications and reroutings and some very fast Class C timings including a non-stop run to York for the 15.15 Scotch Goods ex-King's Cross. Also in 1956 the new 'Talisman' service took up the old 'Coronation' path to Edinburgh, with an interruption from 28 August when the main line was flooded at Granthouse.

The year 1957 was significant for the appear-

Travelling on today's clean, fast, electric main line, we easily forget just how seedy the railway system used to be. Here 'A4' No 60025 *Falcon* appears at the London end of a decidedly scruffy Peterborough North on 17 February 1962. *Philip H. Wells*

This picture of Class 'N2/4' 0-6-2T No 69580 climbing Holloway Bank with the 9.59 am Sunday local to Hatfield on 20 September 1953 typifies an era of London suburban travel on the GN main line. The 'quad-art' sets, of four bodies on five bogies, could hold incredible numbers of commuters in extreme discomfort! *BM*

ance of the first - Type 1 and 2 - diesels, the application of Commonwealth bogies to Mark 1 coaching stock, the start of work on widening the Potters Bar tunnels and the last round of improvements to the 'Pacific' locomotive stud, giving the 'A4s' a double chimney and better steaming properties. At the end of the year, on 18 November, the ER Line organisation was introduced, to be followed by the arrival of the first of the larger diesels, five English Electric 2,000 hp machines allocated to Hornsey depot. On 21 June 1958 D201 worked the down 'Flying Scotsman' to Newcastle, the first scheduled working of an inter-city service by diesel traction. With the order placed for 22 English Electric 3,300 hp Co-Co 'Deltics', the ECML traction scene was changing at last.

When the London Midland won the first cash available for main-line electrification, the East Coast route to Scotland

suffered a period of low morale and indifferent services. The advent of the diesel era was expected to remedy this, but a round of problems with the new motive power in 1959, coupled with disruption resulting from the work taking place between Greenwood and Potters Bar, just served to prolong the agony. There were high-speed runs by the prototype 'Deltic' and by *Sir Nigel Gresley* on an SLS special, but the 'A2/2s' had reached the end of their short road and were condemned.

The 1960s began with the launch of the Anglo Scottish Car Carrier and the completion of AWS throughout to Edinburgh. In February 1961 training began for the production 'Deltics', the first machine arriving at the new Finsbury Park depot not long after. Soon more were appearing, but the first five 'A4s' were condemned, *Silver Link* among them, and by the end of the summer these grand old favourites had worked their last non-stop service over the East Coast Main Line. King's Cross shed was to go in the middle of 1963 once the Class 47s and 55s were fully active.

The era of a high-speed timetable for the ECML began in earnest on 18 June 1962 with the 'Deltics' shouldering the burden of the main services in conjunction with a fleet of Mark I stock on Commonwealth bogies. The 'Tees-Tyne Pullman' was booked at 75.6 mph between Darlington and York to produce the first ever start-to-stop timing of more than 75 mph. On 29 October 1963 the 'A4s' finally bowed out with a last trip by No 60017 on the 18.40 to Leeds, and steam itself would end on Christmas Eve two years later.

The whole character of the East Coast Main Line was now changing. Wholesale cuts in the traditional express fish services were part of a move towards larger wagons, dedicated freight services for single customers and an end to small goods depots and single wagon loads; most of the smaller stations had already been closed to passengers. Significant in this whole process was the commencement of the first Freightliner service from King's Cross on 31 October 1966.

The traditional flat crossing at Retford was replaced by a dive-under to take the merry-go-round traffic to West Burton, and Lincoln services were routed via Newark following the Honington-Lincoln and East Lincs closures. Not only were more paths becoming available, but also steady improvements in the permanent way saw the emergence of the first sections that could be traversed at 100 mph. By the beginning of 1967 the 100 mph signs applied to 77 miles of the route from King's Cross to Edinburgh. The same year brought the last of the fish services and the first of the air-braked trains.

May 1968 was notable for the full implementation of the concept of providing a fast and frequent service by using 'Deltics' hauling only eight coaches. The idea, which had much in common with that behind the 'Silver Jubilee' and 'Coronation' services, had been tried out to the West Riding in April 1966 and had now come into its own as a result of the completion of a preliminary round of track alignment improvements, which put more stretches into the high-speed category. This was to be followed by approval for straightening out the curves down by the Ouse at Offord, for a new alignment at Newton Hall and for other improvements at Grantham, Bawtry and Durham. There was a moment of nostalgia in 1968 when No 4472 *Flying Scotsman* was used on a seven-coach train to commemorate the 40th anniversary of non-stop running to Edinburgh, but the locomotive needed two tenders as only three sets of water troughs remained.

The 1970s started off with the completion of the Stage One improvements to elevate over half the distance to Newcastle to the 95/100 mph standard, and with the approval of the King's Cross-Sandy resignalling scheme. On 12 July 1971 Mark IId air-conditioned coaches came into service, and although all-Pullman trains were phased out, the Government did approve the GN suburban electrification proposals (Moorgate-Welwyn Garden City and King's Cross-Royston). By the following year train names were back in favour with the 'Flying Scotsman', 'Aberdonian' and 'Talisman' plus three Pullmans. Soon these would be running through a remodelled Peterborough and other modified sections which brought 80 per cent of the line to Newcastle up to the 100 mph standard; by 1976 this figure was 89 per cent.

Then, on 12 June 1973, the prototype HST topped a series of high-speed achievements by recording 143.2 mph between York and Darlington. Here was a new dawn featuring a production order for Class 254 HSTs, completion of the Stage 2 alterations (King's Cross area, Peterborough, Grantham, Selby and Darlington-Newcastle), a start on Stage 3 to give the new trains a 125 mph trackbed and, on the extension of the new generation of signalling panels, to push modern regulation north to Doncaster.

A partial Moorgate-Welwyn Garden City suburban electric service in 1976 was extended in 1977, with outer-suburban Class 312 EMUs joining their inner-suburban Class 313 counterparts, and taking over from the Royston DMUs completely in January 1978. By now the production HSTs were being delivered to a new Heaton and extended Bounds Green depots, and the King's Cross area resignalling was complete. Associated changes included a new rolling-stock depot at Hornsey, 'throat' simplification at King's Cross, a new flyover at Welwyn Garden City and a new role as Up Slow for the old freight flyover at Holloway. To mark the 25th anniversary of the Queen's accession, on 8 June 1977 a 'Deltic' had worked a special 'Silver Jubilee' service to Edinburgh in 5 hours 35 minutes, but soon demonstration HST runs gave way to crew training and finally to a limited public service - the 07.45 to Edinburgh and back from 20 March 1978.

The May 1978 timetable was notable for the introduction of eight HST 125 mph services on the East Coast Main Line, among them the 'Flying Scotsman', which reached Edinburgh in less than 5 hours. The services were extended in the following year when the 'Deltics' were relegated to Hull trains and York semi-fasts. Significant changes took place at Doncaster as the 1970s ended, including work on the new control centre and a remodelling that included the old freight yards and the use of the ex-Dearne Valley route at Black Carr as a flyover for the GN&GE Joint line. After track lowering in Stoke and Peascliffe Tunnels to permit the use of the ECML for ISO containers a serious cave-in occurred during reconstruction work on Penmanshiel Tunnel, which had to be remedied by building a new deviation in the open.

By 1980 the 'Deltic' withdrawals had started and HSTs were getting to York in 111 minutes, an average of 101.8 mph. Among the civil engineering news was the commencement of the Selby Diversion, creating an entirely new section of main line between Temple Hirst and Colton junctions, cutting out the traditional slowing for the Ouse swing-bridge and releasing the area north of Selby for a vast new coalfield on completion in 1983. The following year was marked by the approval of the Secretary of State for Transport of a £306 million scheme of electrification to Edinburgh, already being reached in 4½ hours.

A new record was established on 27 September 1985 when a media trip to herald a new 'Tees-Tyne Pullman' service broke the world long-distance diesel traction record by covering 268.6 miles at an average of 115.4 mph. In the process the speedometer touched 144 mph just south of Essendine. But this was almost a swansong, for a

year later GEC was given a contract for 31 Class 91 electric locomotives, and by the November electrification work was sufficiently advanced for EMU services to work through to Huntingdon. From 11 May 1987 there was an hourly electric service between King's Cross and Peterborough.

Using the accumulated experience of earlier electrification schemes, work on changing the face of the East Coast Main Line proceeded rapidly and efficiently to permit energisation to Leeds in 1988, to York in 1989, to Northallerton in mid-1990 and finally through to Edinburgh. At the same time the completion of locomotives and new Mk IV coaching sets, along with trials, training, timetabling and a hundred other facets, were all moving forward on schedule.

In March 1989 the first Class 91-hauled service ran to Leeds, and suburban services benefited from the arrival of Class 317 units to replace the suburban 312s. A press trip with a Class 91 locomotive and Mark IV stock recorded 132 mph on 20 September 1989, and the succeeding two years saw full electrification benefits extended first to York and Newcastle and finally to Scotland. On 12 June 1991 the 11.00 ex-King's Cross inaugurated the InterCity 225 service to Edinburgh.

In company with the train service improvements, major remodelling schemes had streamlined the old and renowned diamond track crossing area at Newcastle and simplified the station layout at York. On 26 September 1991 No 91012 with five vehicles and a DVT showed just what could be achieved from all this by averaging 112.9 mph to Edinburgh, while on 2 June 1995 No 91031 set up a new speed record of 155 mph.

Today the East Coast Main Line is Britain's premier rail route, electrified through to Edinburgh at a cost of over £300 million to provide a speed and quality of service that even the go-ahead Directors of the Great Northern and LNER companies would not have believed possible. The route has been completely remodelled with track layouts straightened and simplified, stations rebuilt and refurbished and other structures given improved clearances. Electric control rooms at Hornsey, Doncaster and Cathcart oversee the power supplies, there are the most up-to-date signalling panels at King's Cross, Doncaster, York and Newcastle, and stock servicing is handled by fully equipped depots at Bounds Green and Heaton. Tyne Yard may be a shadow of its former self, Doncaster Decoy quite empty of coal wagons and Grantham and Top Shed without their 'A4s', but the service and services that have replaced them represent an excellent exchange.

THE EAST COAST MAIN LINE

King's Cross to Newcastle: the route of the 'Silver Jubilee'

1.
'THE CROSS'

Over a nine-week period at the beginning of 1977 the 'throat' at King's Cross was completely remodelled, involving many services terminating at Finsbury Park. *BR*

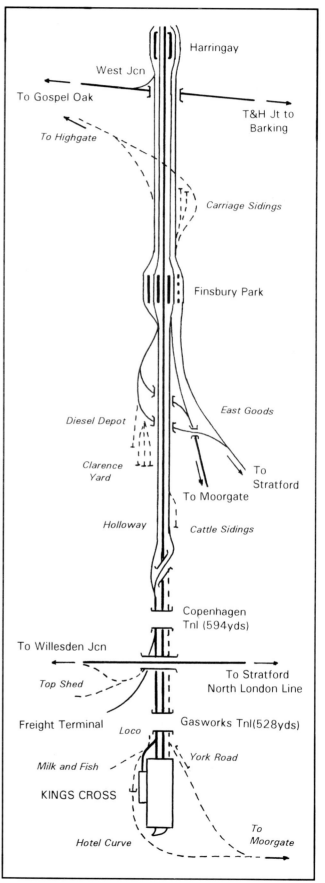

King's Cross and Belle Isle

KING'S CROSS: A scene typical of the LNER 'streamliner' era with two 'A4' streamlined locomotives standing in the great train sheds with a typical LNER signal box presiding over the operation. Pride of place is taken by No 2512 *Silver Fox* setting off with the 5.30 pm 'Silver Jubilee' service to Newcastle. The locomotive, which carries a fox emblem above the valances, is in Garter blue, although its train is in a silver-grey finish. To the right No 4495 *Golden Fleece*, on the 5.45 pm departure, will take 85 minutes longer to get to Newcastle.

In the 1993 view there is less track on the ground but a lot of overhead equipment in the air. Class '47/4' No 47833 in original green livery sets off on 28 January with the 12.20 ARPS special to Peterborough after being named *Captain Peter Manisty RN. E. R. Wethersett/BM*

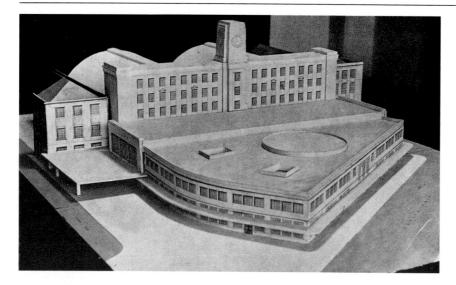

KING'S CROSS: Lewis Cubitt provided the Great Northern Railway with plans for a London terminus that would be both simple and striking, the only concession to elegance being an Italianate clock tower between the two great roof spans. The station opened on 14 October 1852, taking over from a temporary terminus at Maiden Lane that had served since the main line had opened to Peterborough two years earlier. The Cubitt edifice has since gone on to serve passengers starting or completing a journey on the East Coast Main Line with quiet and unassuming efficiency for well over a century, although at one time the clutter of buildings around the station was so great as to earn the soubriquet 'The African Jungle'. In 1946 this 'suggested re-design of King's Cross (architect's model)' was featured in the LNER's five-year plan publication *Forward*, and makes an interesting comparison with the accompanying 1989 view.

The latter shows clearly the improvements made to simplify access and accommodate modernised ticketing and retail facilities. The main station offices, and one-time headquarters offices of the Great Northern Railway, are ranged along the left-hand side of the station, with the suburban station beyond. Ahead of that is the frontage of the Great Northern Hotel. Also designed by Lewis Cubitt, the hotel was opened in 1854. *LNER/BM*

The interior of King's Cross is basically as functional as the exterior, although modern signing and other improvements have helped to offset the original severity. The Great Northern Railway had an excellent reputation for its stock, punctuality and passenger care, but it was not given to architectural frills or any other infrastructure extravagance. In this view, taken on 8 June 1977, only the ornately supported clock has any claim to be decorative. Perhaps it is the train that really matters, in this case the up 'Hull Pullman', which has just arrived behind Class 55 English Electric 'Deltic' locomotive No 55021 *Argyll & Sutherland Highlander*. *BM*

KING'S CROSS: This view of a still very traditional King's Cross captures the period of the 'Deltic' high-speed concept as No 55018 *Ballymoss* pulls out of the station with a standard eight-coach formation. The date is 12 June 1975 and the train the 11.25 departure to Leeds. Behind the dramatic Cubitt train sheds can be seen the Great Northern Hotel and the tall Gothic exuberance of St Pancras.

Gone is the old signal box, but on 22 October 1994 the station remains equally busy with no fewer than four Class 91s and their trains and two Res Class 90 locomotives. *Both BM*

KING'S CROSS: Seen here drawing into King's Cross in July 1938, Gresley 'A4' Class No 4492 *Dominion of New Zealand* has left Leeds at 11.31 am and taken 164 minutes for the 185¾-mile journey. The train is the 'West Riding Limited', labelled in the timetable 'Supplementary Charges - Limited Seating Accommodation - Seats Bookable in Advance', while the locomotive is one of the five originally built for the 'Coronation' services. Back in 1847 George Hudson, the 'Railway King', had signed an agreement that gave the Great Northern Railway its first access to Leeds. This was a major triumph, the more significant because Leeds was the Chairman's home town, and West Riding traffic has been an important feature of the East Coast Main Line movements ever since. Behind the train is the gloom of York Road platform on the line to Moorgate.

York Road finally closed on 5 March 1977 and, like the LNER signal box, has gone completely in the view of the departing 15.00 InterCity service to Glasgow Central on 13 November 1994. The power unit, Class 91 No 91031 *Sir Henry Royce*, is already in Gasworks Tunnel. *W. S. Garth (Rail Archive Stephenson)/BM*

"WEST RIDING LIMITED"

Since their inception the L.N.E.R streamline train services between London and Newcastle ("The Silver Jubilee") and London and Edinburgh ("The Coronation") have won their place in the list of the world's most famous trains. With every confidence in the public patronage of further services of this character, combining high speed with high standard of comfort and punctuality, the London & North Eastern Railway Company introduced the "West Riding Limited" between London, Leeds and Bradford.

The times of departure and arrival are :—

Bradford (Exchange)	dep.	11.10 a.m.
Leeds (Central)	dep.	11.31 a.m.
London (King's Cross)	arr.	2.15 p.m.
London (King's Cross)	dep.	7.10 p.m.
Leeds (Central)	arr.	9.53 p.m.
Bradford (Exchange)	arr.	10.15 p.m.

(See pages 10 and 11 for Mileage Tables.)

The "West Riding Limited" is intended for the use of passengers to and from London only.

3

KING'S CROSS: Still elegant despite the grime, Gresley 'V2' Class 2-6-2 No 60847 *St Peter's School York AD627* emerges from Gasworks Tunnel into King's Cross on 19 July 1952. It has hauled 'The Tynesider' service from Newcastle and was photographed from York Road platform. Developed from Sir Nigel Gresley's LNER 'Pacific' engines, the 'V2' was a heavy mixed-traffic locomotive with good riding qualities and a high performance profile. These locomotives were well loved by their footplatemen and railway devotees alike.

In use for the day as a 'Thunderbird' rescue locomotive for recalcitrant Class 91s, Res Class 47/4 *Restive* stands on the King's Cross blocks on 22 October 1994 and effectively blocks the view of Gasworks Tunnel. *Both BM*

KING'S CROSS SHED: There was never any room to spare at King's Cross loco depot (34A) as this view of the running shed makes clear. On the left on 3 October 1954 is Class 'A4' No 60005 *Sir Charles Newton* with its smokebox panel raised, with 'A4' No 60008 *Dwight D. Eisenhower* nearest the camera; the former was originally *Capercaillie* and No 60008 was *Golden Shuttle*. Behind the latter stands 'B1' Class 4-6-0 No 61144.

In great contrast, the scene on 22 October 1994 shows only grabs, crushers and elevators turning the residue of demolished buildings into hardcore. No trace of 'Top Shed' and its mixture of heat, grime and magic remains. *Both BM*

KING'S CROSS SHED: To commemorate the centenary of Doncaster Works the 'Plant Centenarian' special from Leeds via Doncaster to King's Cross on 27 September 1953 was hauled by 'C1' and 'C2' Class 'Atlantics' Nos 990 *Henry Oakley* and 251. Having arrived at King's Cross 3 minutes early, the two engines have been shunt released and stand in Top Shed recovering from their exertions. Now in the care of the National Railway Museum, both locomotives are notable, *Henry Oakley* as H. A. Ivatt's first British 'Atlantic' and No 251 as an example of the class of 94 GNR 'Large Atlantics' that dominated express workings on the main line until the Gresley 'Pacifics' appeared.

Glamour is notably absent from the same location on 22 October 1994. The road bridge, a few older houses and just one solitary track are all that remain. *Both BM*

KING'S CROSS GOODS: At one time the whole area between Goods Way and York Way was occupied by King's Cross Goods, a vast spread of lines, sheds, cranes and motor vehicles handling every conceivable type of freight from small consignments to container loads. Freightliner traffic, building material terminals and other specialised functions occupied the depot's later years, although it closed for general freight on 5 March 1973. Just 17 days later Class 08 No D3876 is pictured with a load of mineral wagons while Class 31/2 No 5612 passes by.

Currently the background buildings and tip of the church steeple are still there, along with the road bridge, but all the lines on the left have been removed and the trackbed lowered to the level of the main line where the rear of Class 317/0 No 317015, forming the 09.38 Letchworth to Kings Cross, passes. *Both BM*

BELLE ISLE: A little to the left of the previous views, at main line level, we see Class 'B17' 4-6-0 No 61652 *Darlington*, one of 25 locomotives of this class named after football teams; the earlier members of the class largely carried names of country houses. In this shot *Darlington* is working a King's Cross-Cambridge semi-fast service, blasting up the 1 in 107 gradient between Gasworks and Copenhagen tunnels on 27 September 1953.

With the demise of steam has gone the perpetual haze over the lines outside King's Cross, and Class 313 EMU No 313059 forming the 09.35 Welwyn Garden City-King's Cross approaches Gasworks Tunnel in much cleaner air. The line it is using is now the Up Slow or No 2 Slow (although it can be used in either direction), and the embankment on the right of the 'past' view has been removed. *Both BM*

BELLE ISLE: The 12.18 pm King's Cross to Newcastle express passes under the North London line viaduct, which crosses the East Coast Main Line between Gasworks and Copenhagen tunnels. The date is Sunday 13 July 1952 and the locomotive Gresley 'A3' 'Pacific' No 60056 *Centenary*, which was built in 1925 (the centenary of the Stockton & Darlington Railway) as an 'A1' and rebuilt in 1944. The leading coach also boasts Gresley origins.

In the second view Craven Class 105 DTC No E56132 works a local stopping service on 23 March 1973.

Subsequently both former Up and Down Fast lines were taken up in favour of the four east-side tracks. In the third photograph, taken on 22 October 1994, the 11.30 North London Railways service from Stratford Low Level to Richmond passes overhead, formed of a Class 313 EMU. *All BM*

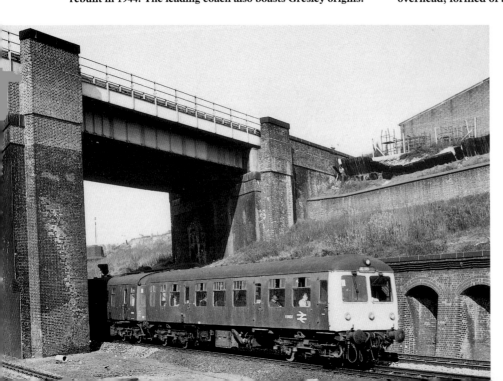

Holloway Bank

HOLLOWAY: King's Cross and its approaches experienced near continuous modernisation work during the 1970s. This picture, taken on 20 November 1976 looking towards the northern portals of Copenhagen Tunnel, gives a good idea of both the remodelling work and the problems of keeping the traffic moving while it took place.

Just how do you protect a train from a shower of 'readimix'? The trains in question are the 08.30 Leeds-King's Cross behind Class 47/4 No 47551 and a down empty stock working headed by Class 31/4 No 31422. The flyover carried the access line for freight trains and trips heading from the up side to King's Cross goods yards and depot. *BM*

Left Seen from this closer angle, looking north, the replacement concrete flyover does gain a little credit for symmetry. Workmen are putting the finishing touches to it on 8 June 1977 as a Cleethorpes-King's Cross train passes beneath powered by Class 46 No 46025. Introduced in 1961 the Class 46 machines were the ultimate form of the 'Peak' Class, but they were eclipsed by the Class 47s and only 56 were built.

Apart from the flyover Holloway is now just plain track, but in LNER days the area boasted four signal boxes and extensive cattle sidings between North Up and South Up boxes. It was also the home of Motorail services for a time. *BM*

HOLLOWAY: Turning the clock back almost 25 years, we see Peppercorn 'A1' 'Pacific' No 60114 *W. P. Allen* emerging from Copenhagen Tunnel on 11 May 1954 at the head of the 5.35 pm King's Cross-Newcastle service. Built at Doncaster, 60114 entered traffic in August 1948, the first of a new class of express engines for the East Coast Main Line. The trackside shrubs in front of the train are a reminder of the LNER's pioneer attempts to improve the railway landscape in this way.

By 1973 the shrubs have gone and Class 55 'Deltic' No 9007 *Pinza* now represents the prime East Coast motive power. The date is 12 September and the train the 17.30 service to the West Riding. Above it Class 31 No 5800 and an electrification train return to their base in the King's Cross yards.

Weeds provide the only trackside adornment in the current picture of Class 91 No 91004 (subsequently named *The Red Arrows*) propelling the 10.30 Leeds-King's Cross beneath the now weather-stained replacement concrete flyover. *BM(2)/ Ken Brunt*

Looking in the other direction, 'J50/3' 0-6-0T No 68949 drifts down Holloway Bank with a freight for King's Cross goods depot on 11 May 1954. *BM*

HOLLOWAY: Gresley 'V2' No 60877 blasts out of Copenhagen Tunnel on 11 July 1953 hauling a King's Cross-Hull service.

Fourteen years later, on 8 June 1977, the gantry signal and fogsignalman's hut have gone, the overhead wires are up and in use, and the King's Cross area resignalling scheme is nearing completion. Civil engineering staff are clearing up the debris as Class 31/1 No 31224 passes with a down Hitchin semi-fast.

By 23 July 1989 one pair of tracks has gone and the vegetation has grown considerably. The same camera position has been used to record the passage of InterCity 125 power car No 43090 at the head of the 13.00 HST service to Edinburgh. *All BM*

HOLLOWAY: Now turning the camera to look north away from Copenhagen Tunnel, we see Peppercorn 'A2' Class 4-6-2 No 60533 *Happy Knight*, built at Doncaster five years earlier, nearing the end of its journey on an up Peterborough train on 29 June 1953.

Twenty years later, on 22 March 1973, what was then Class 31/2 No 5568 descends Holloway Bank towards Copenhagen Tunnel with one of the Cambridge Buffet Express services; these trains carried headcode 1B66 in both directions.

Today the two chimneys on the skyline and the building in the right distance remain, otherwise it is all change as the 13.09 from Welwyn Garden City, formed of Class 317/1 EMU No 317347, crosses the flyover that now carries the Up Slow line to the down side. Even the church steeple has gone. *All BM*

MAIN LINE—LONDON TO YORK.

Block working.	Distance from King's × passenger station. Miles	Chns.	Distance from King's Cross goods station / from Canonbury junction	Stations, sidings and signal boxes.	Distance from point to point. Miles	Chns.	Shunting sidings. Down.	Up.	Closed	Stations to which the signal boxes and sidings are attached.
Absolute.	..	..		King's Cross passgr. station	..	..	..	..	..	King's × Passenger.
	..	15		,, east box .. .. (signals up lines only)	..	15	..	..	..	
	..	16½		,, west box .. .. (signals down lines and up carriage road)	..	1½	..	..	..	
	..	17¾		,, jun with up sub. line	..	1¼	..	..	..	
	..	19¾		,, York Road station	..	2	..	..	..	
	..	21½		,, junction with down suburban line ..	..	1¾	..	..	..	
	..	49		,, Belle Isle down box ‡ (signals down lines only)	..	27½	..	..	..	
	..	57¼		,, Belle Isle up box ‡ (signals up lines only)	..	8¼	..	..	..	
	..	63¾		Copenhagen junction box ‡ (signals down lines and Belle Isle siding only)	..	6½	..	..	..	
	..	65		,, junction	..	1¼	..	..	..	
	..	..		King's Cross goods stn.	..	..	..	..	..	..
				,, gds. & min.	..	..	..	..	..	King's × Passenger.
	..	..	.. 31¼	junction box.. ..	..	31¼	..	..	..	
	..	..	.. 32¼	Jn. to Frederick st. gds. yd	..	¾	..	..	..	
	..	..	.. 34½	Branch to N. L. R. jun.	..	2¼	..	..	..	
	..	..	.. 39	Copenhagen junction box	..	4½	..	..	..	
	..	..	.. 40¼	,, junction ..	..	1¼	..	..	..	
	1	32	.. ..	Holloway south down ‡ (signals down line only)	..	47	..	..	..	Holloway.
	1	33	.. ..	Holloway south up box ‡ (signals up lines only)	..	1	..	..	..	
	1	39	.. ..	Islingt'n Borough Electric Light siding	..	6	..	..	..	
	1	41½	.. ..	Holloway cattle branch junction	..	2½	..	..	..	
	..	..	.. 18¾	Holloway cattle station	..	18¾	..	..	..	
	1	43½		Holloway & Caled'n Rd. stn. (Distance from Cattle branch junction)	..	2	..	..	..	Do.
	1	51¾		,, carriage sidings box ..	..	8¼	..	..	..	
	1	53¾		,, north up box .. .. (signals up lines only)	..	2	..	..	..	
	1	60¼		,, north down box .. (signals down lines only)	..	6½	..	..	..	
	2	5¾		East goods yard box	..	25½	..	..	After shunting is completed Sunday mornings to 8.0 p.m. Sundays	Finsbury Park
	2	12¾		Clarence Yard .. .. .. (Distance from Holloway north down box)	..	32½	..	..	..	
				CANONBURY BRANCH.						
				Canonbury junction ..	..	..	..	..	Worked by N.L. Co.	
	..	..	.. 2¼	,, ,, box	..	2¼	..	..		
	..	..	.. 5¼	Highbury Crescent box ‡	..	3	..	..	..	Do.
	..	..	.. 37¾	Drayton Park box.. ‡	..	32½	..	..	..	
	..	..	.. 38½	Ashburton goods Yd. jct. (Dist. from Finsbury P'k, box 1)	..	¾	..	..	..	
	..	..	.. 52¼	Highbury Vale goods Yd.	..	13¾	..	..	..	
	..	..	.. 55½	Finsbury Park box 1 ..	..	3¼	..	..	..	

Details of signal boxes in the King's Cross/Holloway area from the GNR 1912 General Appendix.

HOLLOWAY: A suburban comparison between 1981 and 1994: on 2 June of the former year four-car Class 312/0 set No 312716 is in use on the 10.40 King's Cross to Royston service. These units, which started to appear from BREL York in 1975, look quite traditional in style.

The only changes in the scene on 29 October 1994 are in the train, the graffiti and the embankment foliage. The Class 312s have been replaced by Class 317s, and here No 317372 climbs away from Copenhagen Tunnel on its diagram as the 08.59 King's Cross-Letchworth service. *Both BM*

Finsbury Park and Harringay

FINSBURY PARK: Holloway Bank is followed by a short, level stretch on the approach to Finsbury Park, but Riddles BR Standard '5MT' 4-6-0 No 73157 is still working hard in this scene captured on 22 April 1958. The locomotive heads a down Cambridge Buffet Express, longer than usual and made up of a mixed bunch of coaches. On the up side a grimy 'N2' 0-6-2T is working 'The Aberdonian' stock into King's Cross, typical of the countless types of job this class of locomotive performed.

On 23 July 1989 one of the buildings in the background remains as the 08.20 Leeds-King's Cross train passes the noon departure from King's Cross to Edinburgh at the summit of Holloway Bank. Class 91 No 91006 propels the service from Leeds, with Class 43 HST power car No 43070 heading the Anglo-Scottish express. Electrification had reached Leeds earlier in the year and was nearing completion on the Doncaster-York stretch. *Both BM*

FINSBURY PARK: The down 'Silver Jubilee' approaches Finsbury Park on 12 July 1937 in the charge of streamlined 'A4' 'Pacific' No 2512 *Silver Fox*. One of the quartet built for that service, 2512 carries a replica of a leaping fox on its boiler casing, a gift to the LNER by United Steel on behalf of its subsidiary Samuel Fox & Co. On the up side a good example of a GNR somersault signal is in the 'off' position, and each of the four posts on the gantry is topped by a GN finial.

Among the many changes at Finsbury Park is the fact that it is now on the route of the electric service to Kings Lynn, the destination of this 13.55 service from King's Cross on 13 November 1994. The Class 317/2 unit is No 317368. *John P. Wilson (Rail Archive Stephenson)/BM*

FINSBURY PARK: A Cravens Class 105 DMU approaches Finsbury Park on 12 March 1972 with a suburban service to King's Cross, passing Class 31 No 5614 on an engineers' train and, behind that, stabled suburban stock. These sidings between the old Highgate branch and the main line used to be the domain of a pretty lively bunch of lady carriage cleaners.

Today the platform extension covers the spot where Finsbury Park No 6 signal box used to be, the nearest bridge has gone and, of course, multiple aspect signalling has replaced the earlier mixture of semaphores and colour lights. On 5 November 1994 the 12.05 InterCity service from Leeds to King's Cross passes the same spot, Mk 4 DVT No 82225 leading and Class 91 No 91006, as yet unnamed, in the rear. *Brian Beer/BM*

FINSBURY PARK: No 55007 *Pinza* is pictured outside Finsbury Park diesel depot on 15 January 1977; although not as well groomed as it might be, the powerful and pleasing appearance of this locomotive provides an idea of just why these English Electric machines, with their two 18-cylinder Napier 1,650 bhp 'Deltic' engines, were so well respected. The diesel depot site was once part of Clarence Yard where express freight trains from King's Cross depot picked up before speeding off north.

After the diesel depot closed the site lay derelict for a time but was finally cleared to make way for a new housing estate. From the same camera position on 30 October 1994 only a colour light signal on the other side of the wall indicates that railway activity continues. *Both BM*

HARRINGAY: The year 1937 must have been really something in the railway world with a new streamlined train to capture the imagination and new streamlined locomotives to look for, discuss and enthuse over. Despite the dangers of their position, these youngsters are completely engrossed in the sight of the down 'Coronation' service picking up speed as it passes Harringay at the beginning of its 268½-mile journey to Newcastle. Class 'A4' streamlined 'Pacific' No 4489 *Dominion of Canada* heads the train.

No footbridge now for the boys to sit on and watch the trains go by, but the background houses appear remarkably unchanged on 22 October 1994 as Class 91 No 91013 *Michael Faraday* approaches Harringay hauling the 17.00 InterCity service from King's Cross to Glasgow Central. *W. S. Garth (Rail Archive Stephenson)/BM*

2.
NORTH
THROUGH
WOOD GREEN

A 1949 advert reminding the nation of the importance of rail-borne freight traffic in post-war Britain.

Each and every day — the year throughout

Raw materials, finished products, the food you eat, the clothes you wear — so many requirements of everyday life — depend largely on rail transport.

BRITISH RAILWAYS

Linking supply with demand

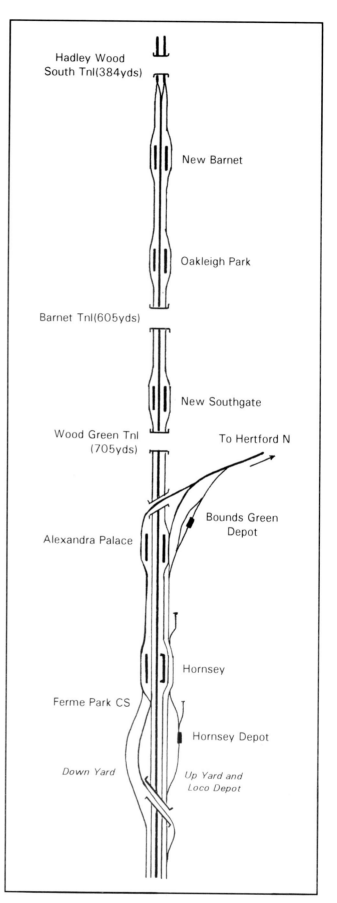

Hadley Wood South Tnl(384yds)

New Barnet

Oakleigh Park

Barnet Tnl(605yds)

New Southgate

Wood Green Tnl (705yds)

To Hertford N

Bounds Green Depot

Alexandra Palace

Hornsey

Ferme Park CS

Hornsey Depot

Down Yard

Up Yard and Loco Depot

Ferme Park and Hornsey

FERME PARK: Crossing over the main line between Harringay and Hornsey, Class 'J52/2' 0-6-0ST No 68846 heads a mixed freight for the North London line on 5 October 1957. This is still the era of the small wagon, with the Esso tanks at the front of the train followed by Conflats, then examples of Open and Boxvan types. In the adjoining Ferme Park up and down yards this incredible sort of mixture would be equally evident, together with all the other paraphernalia of moving goods traffic - brake vans, cattle pens, loading docks, load gauges, shunting poles, tail lamps and the like.

With the viaduct completely rebuilt and the track alignment altered, the present-day scene at this location bears little resemblance to the previous photograph. It shows Class 43 power car No 43119 passing beneath the new flyover heading empty HST stock from Bounds Green depot to King's Cross. *Stanley Creer/BM*

For over a hundred years freight earned more revenue for railways than passenger traffic. In those years this vast railway area at Ferme Park would have been filled with wagons being shunted in the up and down yards. In the up yard, which used to be on the right-hand side of this picture, coal trains, 'rough' goods, docks and other transfer traffic were the principal occupation, while the down yard dealt mainly with empties. In this photograph, taken on 22 October 1994, the area is entirely devoted to the stabling, servicing and maintenance of passenger rolling-stock, a Class 43 power car taking fuel prior to working into King's Cross to form an Anglo-Scottish HST departure. The view is looking north, with Hornsey station in the middle of the main line's double curve. *BM*

HORNSEY: The up 'Yorkshire Pullman' makes a superb sight as it approaches Hornsey station on 12 March 1962, but the regulator will have been closed as the driver reacts to seeing the Ferme Park Distant signal at Caution. His engine is Class 'A4' No 60007 *Sir Nigel Gresley*, which is well capable of making good this check, despite a 400-ton load, if the delay is not too severe. However, the signalman will have some explaining to do!

On 22 October 1994 the 07.55 Aberdeen-King's Cross HST is led by Class 43 power car No 43086. Although the signal boxes and impressive gantries have gone, the twin gasholders remain, although they, too, have been modernised. *Maurice Edwards/BM*

HORNSEY SHED: Gresley 'J50/4' 0-6-0T No 68991 stands outside Hornsey shed (34B) on a sunny 3 October 1954. First appearing in the last days of the Great Northern Railway, when they were given vacuum brakes for passenger working, the 'J50s' eventually became the standard LNER shunting engine. Thirty of the class were allocated to Hornsey, primarily for working cross-London freight services, and the two seen here stand amid the grime and clutter of the down-to-earth steam shed that was their home.

Much altered to conform to modern standards, the Hornsey steam shed building still survives today and, reroofed, is used as a store for the adjacent Hornsey electric depot. *Both BM*

Shed staff and fitters from the steam age just would not believe that any building connected with rail traction could ever look so clean and orderly. Not only that, but you can actually see what you are doing in this scene at Hornsey Traction Maintenance Depot on 11 February 1990 when Class 313 No 313054, Class 317/2 No 317356 and Battery Loco No 97704 pose for the camera in the six-road building. *BM*

Wood Green and Palace Gates

WOOD GREEN/ALEXANDRA PALACE: Under the windows of Wood Green No 4 signal box Peppercorn Class 'A1' 'Pacific' No 60157 *Great Eastern* hurries south on a New England-King's Cross express parcels on 9 April 1952. This was before the BRUTE system for parcels had imposed a little more uniformity on the process of selecting vehicles for such trains, and the one in the photograph has a very motley collection of vans.

In the second scene the signal box has gone together with the gas lamp and one of the footbridges, and the station now bears the name Alexandra Palace. The outer-suburban service passing in front of the surviving Great Northern Railway booking office is the 10.38 from Letchworth on 5 November 1994 formed of Class 317/1 No 317317. *Both BM*

WOOD GREEN/ALEXANDRA PALACE: On the left can be seen something of the turmoil caused by the relaying work on the main line on 3 October 1976. This meant the diversion of all services via the Hertford Loop, including the 10.35 up express from Newcastle seen here winding its tortuous way down the connecting line from the branch and past Wood Green No 2 signal box to rejoin the main line.

With Bounds Green depot now constructed over the site of the old signal box and the trackwork realigned, this is the view today. Only the houses in the background remain to provide a reference. *Ken Brunt/BM*

PALACE GATES: Just a few steps from Wood Green station was the GE-line branch terminus at Palace Gates, from which a service operated to North Woolwich. The area between the two always housed some peripheral railway activity, but for some years now has been important as the site of Bounds Green maintenance depot. The first photograph pictures Palace Gates on 10 April 1954 with Holden 'F5' Class 2-4-2T No 67209 at the head of a stopping train to North Woolwich.

To take a photograph in the same place today it was necessary to obtain permission from ex-BR driver Vic Powell to use the rear of his house in Braemar Avenue.

The north end of the old Palace Gates station platforms are adjacent to Bounds Green depot (visible in the left distance of the third photograph) and still survive. This area once formed part of a little-used connection between the GN and GE systems, but all that remains on 5 November 1994 is the decaying platforms, two vans and some overgrown track. *All BM*

BOUNDS GREEN: *Above right* This line-up at Bounds Green depot on 17 February 1989 was arranged to show off four different liveries to the BBC *Railwatch* cameras. From left to right the participants were InterCity Class 91 No 91003, Petroleum sub-sector Railfreight Class 37/7 No 37893, General user Class 47/4 No 47625 and Departmental 31/4 No 31412. Bounds Green has grown over the years to become a major feature of the siding and maintenance complex that extends from Harringay to Alexandra Park, and undertakes the remaining locomotive maintenance in addition to the IC sets. *BM*

Right Resulting from electrification of the East Coast Main Line all the Class 91 locomotives and the InterCity fleet of Mk IV stock come to Bounds Green for maintenance, the previous incumbents, the HSTs, having been transferred to Neville Hill and Craigentinny. Inside the depot on 8 August 1991 Class 89 No 89001 *Avocet*, built by BREL Crewe for Hawker Siddeley in 1986, stands ahead of BREL Crewe/GEC Class 91 No 91006, the latter lifted on jacks for attention to the bogies. *BM*

WOOD GREEN TUNNELS: The down 'Heart of Midlothian' service is pictured here on 27 March 1954, just starting the 8-mile climb at 1 in 200 that will bring the train to the summit at Potters Bar. Gresley 'A4' 4-6-2 No 60034 *Lord Faringdon* (formerly *Peregrine*) is in charge of the train, and some 'hunting' between the first and second coach bogies is already noticeable.

In the second view, dated 22 September 1989, the 12.20 King's Cross Yard to Peterborough cement train has left Alexandra Palace and is heading for Wood Green Tunnels. At the front are two Class 31/1s, No 31289 in blue and No 31209 in what was then the latest Railfreight livery but without subsector decals. *Both BM*

WOOD GREEN TUNNELS: Emerging from the centre portal of the 705-yard tunnel on 27 March 1954, Thompson 'L1' Class 2-6-4T No 67785 heads a Royston to King's Cross semi-fast service. These tank engines were built for just such workings, but although nice-looking machines they had a poor reputation. Dropping a piston rod was among their less endearing qualities!

There is more vegetation and a great profusion of overhead metalwork in the second view, taken on 23 September 1989. The train leaving Wood Green Tunnel and heading towards Alexandra Palace is the 10.50 Letchworth to King's Cross formed of Class 317/2 No 317352, still in original blue/grey livery. *Both BM*

Oakleigh Park and New Barnet

OAKLEIGH PARK: With a heavy Doncaster-King's Cross mixed freight in tow, Thompson 'B1' Class 4-6-0 No 61265 drifts downgrade through Oakleigh Park station on 28 February 1953. A Conflat loaded with a B-type container follows the locomotive tender, then three vans, all built to a different profile and a reminder that the original pre-Grouping companies all worked to a slightly different loading gauge.

In the second view, taken on 5 November 1994, the 08.00 Glasgow-King's Cross InterCity services passes through Oakleigh Park at speed. Headed by Mk4 DVT No 82222, power is provided from the rear by Class 91 No 91003 *The Scotsman*. *Both BM*

Approaching New Barnet on the Slow line, Class 58 No 58027 hauls Castle Cement tanks northwards from King's Cross Goods on 19 August 1994, heading for Ketton near Stamford. Forerunners of a new breed of freight traction, the Type 5 Class 58s were built by BREL between 1983 and 1985 and powered with GEC Ruston Paxman engines and Brush traction equipment, giving a potential tractive effort of 60,750 lb. These bulk cement movements had their beginnings back in the late '50s and signalled BR's steady expansion in carryings of aggregates and general building materials. *BM*

OAKLEIGH PARK: Over 17 years old and still going strong, the first Gresley 'A4' 'Pacific', No 60014 *Silver Link*, heads the down 'Heart of Midlothian' near Oakleigh Park on 28 February 1953. No 60014 has changed its appearance since 1935, including the removal of the valances covering the motion, a slight change in the front-end profile, longer buffers, a non-recessed coupling and the fitting of Kylchap double blastpipes and chimneys.

In its own way the train in the modern view is equally impressive. The service is the 13.00 King's Cross-Glasgow Central via Edinburgh, the power is provided by Class 91 No 91022 *Robert Adley*, the scene is again the bank between New Southgate and Oakleigh Park and the date 5 November 1994. The centre main-line tracks have been lowered as part of the electrification works. *Both BM*

OAKLEIGH PARK: The date is 26 July 1979 as 'Deltic' No 55015 *Tulyar* hurries the 10.45 from Leeds through Oakleigh Park. By this time the end is near for these tried and trusted locomotives; already HSTs have taken over many of the principal InterCity services and in 1980 the withdrawal of the 'Deltics' will begin, the engines that survive being relegated to secondary services.

On 5 November a Mk IV DVT approaches Oakleigh Park with the 11.05 Leeds-King's Cross train. Class 91 No 91013 *Michael Faraday* is out of sight at the rear. *BM/Ken Brunt*

NEW BARNET: Although the track layout at New Barnet retains some similarities, every other aspect of these two photographs testifies to the dramatic changes of the last few decades. The LNER signal box has gone, along with the somersault signals and their attendant signal wire and point rodding, and even the telephone lines have disappeared from the poles in favour of fibre-optic cables in lineside ducts. Below the electric current wiring and structures the rails are now flat-bottomed and spiked to concrete sleepers instead of the traditional bullhead design in chairs on wooden sleepers. The proud trains have changed just as much, from one of the newly introduced 'Silver Jubilee' services on 16 July 1937 to a modern InterCity express on 19 August 1994.

In the first illustration the down 'Silver Jubilee' is headed by the streamlined Gresley 'A4' 'Pacific' No 2510 *Quicksilver*, while in the second the 15.00 King's Cross-Edinburgh service is powered by Class 91 No 91025 *BBC Radio 1 FM. John P. Wilson (Rail Archive Stephenson)/BM*

3.
HATFIELD
AND
WELWYN

The LNER's 1946 post-war New Works Programme promised '£1,023,000 - Additional up and down lines between Greenwood (Hadley Wood) and Potters Bar. Reconstruction of Hadley Wood and Potters Bar stations.' In the event the work was not completed until 1955.

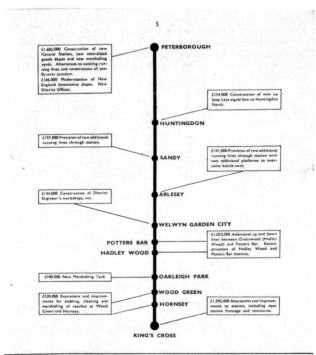

5

£1,682,000 Construction of new Central Station, new centralised goods depot and new marshalling yards. Alterations to existing running lines and construction of new fly-over junction.
£146,000 Modernisation of New England locomotive depot. New District Offices.

£154,000 Construction of new up loop Leys signal box to Huntingdon North.

PETERBOROUGH

HUNTINGDON

£157,000 Provision of two additional running lines through station.

£141,000 Provision of two additional running lines through station with two additional platforms to overcome bottle-neck.

SANDY

£144,000 Construction of District Engineer's workshops, etc.

ARLESEY

WELWYN GARDEN CITY

£1,023,000 Additional up and down lines between Greenwood (Hadley Wood) and Potters Bar. Reconstruction of Hadley Wood and Potters Bar stations.

POTTERS BAR
HADLEY WOOD

£100,000 New Marshalling Yard.

OAKLEIGH PARK

£530,000 Extensions and improvements for stabling, cleaning and marshalling of coaches at Wood Green and Hornsey.

WOOD GREEN
HORNSEY

£1,595,000 Alterations and improvements to station, including new station frontage and concourse.

KING'S CROSS

L·N·E·R NEW WORKS PROGRAMME
EAST COAST MAIN LINE, KING'S CROSS TO PETERBOROUGH

Knebworth

Woolmer Green

Welwyn North Tnl (1046yds)

Welwyn South Tnl (446yds)

Welwyn North

River Mimram

Welwyn Viaduct

To Luton and Dunstable

CS

Digswell

To Hertford N

Welwyn Garden City

To St Albans

Hatfield

Marshmoor

Welham Green

Brookmans Park

Potters Bar

Potters Bar Tnl (1214yds)

Hadley Wood North Tnl(232yds)

Hadley Wood

Hadley Wood and Potters Bar

HADLEY WOOD: Although the pre-war 'Scarborough Flyer' was re-instated for summer weekends in 1950, its post-war schedule hardly justified the epithet 'Flyer'. In this picture the train is leaving the 384-yard Hadley Wood South Tunnel and running through the station on 19 July 1952 with Peppercorn 'A1' Class 4-6-2 No 60122 *Curlew* steaming freely despite the 1 in 200 adverse gradient.

On 7 November 1994 the 11.21 Great Northern Lines service from Peterborough to King's Cross passes through Hadley Wood station at speed, formed of Class 317/2 No 317555. Not only has the old station lost its period booking office, decorated canopy and gaslamps but, resulting from the widening works, the 1994 train is on the Up Fast line which in 1952 was the Down Main. *Both BM*

HADLEY WOOD: It is no longer possible to duplicate exactly this pre-war view of 'A4' No 2509 *Silver Link* with the 'Silver Jubilee' train just north of Hadley Wood. This is because the bank on the right is now occupied by two extra tracks, and the vantage point used by the photographer by the parapet of the additional bore of Hadley Wood North Tunnel. The 'Silver Jubilee', instead of being on the Down Main line, would be speeding along the Up Fast in the down direction!

The train pictured on 7 November 1994 is a Ripple Lane to Immingham service loaded with newsprint and headed by Class 37/7 No 37719. This Type 3 machine was part of a batch built by English Electric in 1961-65 and refurbished by BREL at Crewe in 1986-89.
G. Body collection/BM

HADLEY WOOD: Drifting downgrade towards the capital on 1 July 1952, Class 'A4' No 60030 *Golden Fleece* leaves the short 232-yard Hadley Wood North Tunnel relatively clear of smoke. The 'Pacific' is working an express from Leeds, which is appropriate since she and her sister engine *Golden Shuttle* (later *Dwight D. Eisenhower*) were built for the 1937 'West Riding Limited' and given names appropriate to the area's woollen industry.

The second tunnel was constructed in the 1950s, and on 7 November 1994 Class 313 No 313029 emerges from the original bore and approaches its Hadley Wood stop with the 12.11 stopping service from Welwyn Garden City to Moorgate. *Both BM*

GANWICK: Emerging at speed from the north end of Hadley Wood North Tunnel on 19 July 1952, on the stretch of line between the tunnel and Potters Bar known as Ganwick, Class 'V2' 2-6-2 No 60861 powers the 10.18 King's Cross-Leeds/Bradford express. With a 'V2' up front one never relied upon getting the same performance as with a 'Pacific', but one often did. Despite years of hard work the 'V2s' were great engines, noted for their reliability and toughness and for providing a comfortable footplate ride.

Also bursting out of Hadley Wood North Tunnel, this time on 14 June 1991, the 16.00 King's Cross-Aberdeen 'Aberdonian' HST is headed by Class 43 power car No 43042. Now extended, the building above the tunnel still remains, but has a second bore running beneath it. *Both BM*

GANWICK: Approaching the tunnel, another 'V2', No 60876, heads for King's Cross Goods with a long fitted freight train on 19 July 1952. The locomotive carries Class C headlamps: 'Express freight, livestock, perishable or ballast train piped throughout with automatic vacuum brake operative on not less than half of the vehicles'.

Passing Ganwick on 16 June 1991 the 16.06 Welwyn Garden City-Moorgate 'stopper' is formed of Class 313 EMUs No 313056 and 313026. *Both BM*

POTTERS BAR: *Below* The station is still in its original form on 12 September 1953, but work on the removal of the station footbridge suggests that the reconstruction process has at last started. The boy on the down platform meanwhile waves to Class 'V2' 2-6-2 No 60872 *King's Own Yorkshire Light Infantry* as it passes with a Hull-King's Cross express. *BM*

POTTERS BAR: In the first of this sequence of four views, Gresley 'K3' 'Mogul' No 61811 approaches Potters Bar heading north with a train of B-type freight containers (as featured in the 1949 advert *below left*) on 12 September 1953, before the quadrupling; what might be called a precursor of the present-day Freightliner services. Despite originating back in 1920 the 'K3' 2-6-0 mixed traffic engine in its various forms lasted until the final years of steam, turning its hand to every conceivable type of working. No stranger to the East Coast Main Line, the 'K3' was also known for producing a rhythmic connecting rod noise labelled 'the Gresley knock'.

In the second view (*below right*), with Potters Bar cutting now increased to four tracks, albeit only as far as Potters Bar

Tunnel, Gresley 'B17/4' No 61652 *Darlington* works a down Cambridge Buffet Express on 16 July 1955. The turnout from the Main to Slow lies just beyond the rear coach and a 'trap' guards against runaways on the latter.

By the date of the third picture (*opposite above*), 6 December 1975, quadrupling on through the tunnels has been completed as the 10.04 King's Cross-Royston service, formed of two Class 105 Craven twins led by DMBS No E51273, approaches the scheduled Potters Bar stop.

Finally, the view on 4 November 1989 (*opposite below*) shows the section with overhead electrification equipment added. Class 317/1 No 317335 forms the 13.10 train from King's Cross to Cambridge. *All BM*

Welham Green and Hatfield

WELHAM GREEN: Class 87/1 No 87101 *Stephenson* hauls 20 HEA hoppers on a northbound ECML electrification test train through Welham Green, near Hatfield, on 3 November 1986. This locomotive followed the GEC Class 87/0 machines built for the West Coast Main Line electrification in 1973, but was provided with thyristor control equipment. The siding appears to be all that remains of the access to Marshmoor Yard and the former Mowlem's private sidings, Marshmoor signal box having completely disappeared.

On 10 September 1994 Class 91 No 91001 *Swallow* passes the same location leading a King's Cross-Newcastle InterCity express. Now new electrical boxes are in position and the old siding connection has been removed. *Both Ken Brunt*

HATFIELD: On 14 January 1978 the 14.30 King's Cross-Cambridge train is formed of two-car Metro-Cammell Class 101 and Cravens Class 105 DMUs, the former in the short-lived experimental off-white livery with blue stripe. On the down side Hatfield used to have a small loco depot for the 'N2s' and other engines that worked its branch services to St Albans and to Dunstable, and Hertford North via Welwyn Garden City.

Today little seems to have changed since the 1978 view although the sidings on the right have been taken up and the surroundings appear a lot more verdant. On 15 October 1994 a local service for King's Cross departs from the main platform formed of Class 313 No 313020, while Class 317/2 No 317357 making up a Cambridge-King's Cross train rapidly overtakes. *BM/Ken Brunt*

HATFIELD: Heading south through the station on 14 January 1978, an unidentified Class 31 hauls the 13.30 Cambridge-King's Cross train. Behind it is the site of the old goods depot that never dealt with much but coal traffic once the railhead was set up at nearby Welwyn Garden City.

By the time of the second view on 15 October 1994 the former goods depot has found a new function as a car park and there are several new buildings in the background. On the tracks Class 317/2 No 317357 passes the station at speed with the 16.28 service from Cambridge to King's Cross. *Both BM*

HATFIELD: Helped by the down gradient of 1 in 200 from Welwyn Garden City, the up 'Flying Scotsman' passes through Hatfield at speed on 14 January 1978. The train is in the charge of Class 55 'Deltic' No 55012 *Crepello*, yet another locomotive carrying on a tradition of bearing the name of a notable racehorse. On the section between Hatfield and Welwyn Garden City an extra single line on both the down and up sides used to carry the Dunstable and Hertford North trains (respectively), and these were operated as single lines rather than as adjuncts to the main line.

The second view is of the noon departure from Edinburgh to King's Cross on 15 October 1994. A Mk IV DVT leads and power is provided from the rear by out-of-view Class 91 No 91016. *Both BM*

Welwyn Garden City

WELWYN GARDEN CITY: The station at Welwyn Garden City, serving the second of Ebenezer Howard's model towns, was not opened until 20 September 1926 and its architecture reflected both that of the town itself and of the period. A bad railway accident in the vicinity on 15 June 1935 resulted in a modification of signalling practice that came to be known as Welwyn Block. In the first view empty stock to form the 16.27 to Moorgate arrives at Welwyn Garden City from the sidings on 22 March 1982. Class 313 unit No 313005 was among those subsequently transferred to Bletchley for North Western Lines.

The 15.21 Peterborough-King's Cross semi-fast service passes Welwyn Garden City on 15 October 1994 formed of Class 317/1 No 317307. The car parking area is now embodied in the 'Howardsgate' shopping complex, which also embraces the main station entrance. *Both BM*

In the years after the war the main GN line inner-suburban services from Moorgate, Broad Street and King's Cross turned round at New Barnet, but the spread of commuting has been such that this role is now filled by Welwyn Garden City, provided with extra sidings and a flyover for the task. The station has an off-peak service of four trains an hour, two ex-Moorgate terminating plus two ex-King's Cross for Cambridge and Peterborough. The photograph shows the 16.35 service to Moorgate formed of Class 313 No 313040 heading for the flyover to get to the upside tracks on 15 October 1994. *BM*

WELWYN VIADUCT: At Digswell Emergency Crossover, 21 miles 20 chains from King's Cross, the East Coast Main Line encounters its first bottleneck as the four tracks reduce to two for the passage over Welwyn Viaduct. As can be seen from the first photograph, engineers Sir William and Joseph Cubitt opted for a very plain affair and the modest River Mimram below does no more to impress. Seen from river level, however, the structure is a different creature, rising 100 feet and provided with 40 arches to span the wide green valley. Class 'V2' 2-6-2 No 60866 also looks impressive as it returns to New England with a long train of coal empties on 17 April 1954.

In the second photograph the electrification gantries have increased the plainness factor, but the valley has acquired a magical air in the afternoon mist. The train on the viaduct on 14 October 1994 is the 15.30 King's Cross-Newcastle led by Class 91 No 91006. *Both BM*

WELWYN NORTH: The 'WD' locomotives were built in 1943 to a Riddles Ministry of Supply design labelled 'Austerity' because of its basic simplicity. They were purchased by the newly formed national railway system in 1948 and classified '8F'. Well over 700 were operational at one period, including No 90158 seen here passing Welwyn North on 17 April 1954 with a Class H freight from Ferme Park to Grantham.

Despite some cosmetic work Welwyn North 40 years later is still clearly a no-frills Great Northern station. The upside staff building has a new roof, the platform a new seat and electricity has taken over from gas as well as steam, but there is no mistaking the origins of the station house, the footbridge and the platform canopy. The train is the 15.08 King's Cross-Cambridge semi-fast slowing for its stop on 14 October 1994 and formed of Class 317/2 No 317362. *Both BM*

WELWYN TUNNELS: North of the broad, shallow valley of the River Mimram the route of the original Great Northern Railway encountered an area of higher ground. Two tunnels and a further 1 in 200 gradient rise were employed to deal with this, Welwyn South and North tunnels remaining as part of the first two-track section of the ECML since leaving King's Cross. The 'past' photograph shows the down 'White Rose' service bursting from the 446-yard South Tunnel on 17 April 1954. At its head is Peppercorn Class 'A1' 'Pacific' No 60141 *Abbotsford*, one of the Darlington 1948 build.

With the trees on the hillside having proliferated to the near forest category, but with everything else seemingly little changed, Class 89 No 89001 emerges from Welwyn South Tunnel on 19 January 1988 heading the 10.15 driver training service from Hornsey to Peterborough and back. *Both BM*

WELWYN TUNNELS: Another down steam service bursting from Welwyn South Tunnel and soon to plunge into the 1,046 yards of the second, North, tunnel. Just beyond that, at Woolmer Green, the train will end the serious climbing until it reaches Stoke Bank, south of Grantham and still some 60 miles ahead. On 17 April 1954 Class 'A4' No 60013 *Dominion of New Zealand* seems to be steaming freely at the head of its King's Cross-Leeds/Bradford train and to be taking the rising gradient in its stride. On the adjacent up freight someone has left a bolster on the 'Bobol' in a bit of a sorry state.

The freight working pictured on 22 March 1982 is a train of sand empties from King's Cross Yard to Fen Drayton. The engine is Class 37/0 No 37077. *Both BM*

4.
HERTFORDSHIRE INTO BEDFORDSHIRE

East Bedfordshire is a prominent market gardening area, and in steam days important northbound express freight services such as 'The Five-Fifteen North Eastern' made stops at Biggleswade and Sandy to pick up traffic (see page 82).

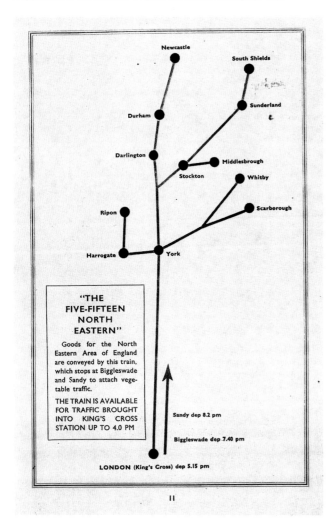

"THE FIVE-FIFTEEN NORTH EASTERN"

Goods for the North Eastern Area of England are conveyed by this train, which stops at Biggleswade and Sandy to attach vegetable traffic.

THE TRAIN IS AVAILABLE FOR TRAFFIC BROUGHT INTO KING'S CROSS STATION UP TO 4.0 PM

Sandy dep 8.2 pm

Biggleswade dep 7.40 pm

LONDON (King's Cross) dep 5.15 pm

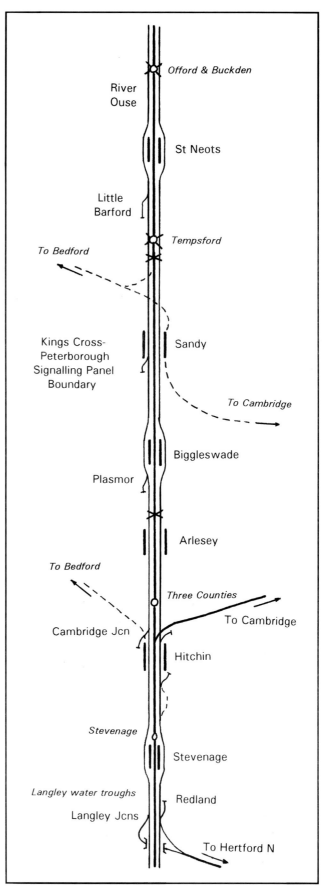

Offord & Buckden
River Ouse
St Neots
Little Barford
To Bedford
Tempsford
Kings Cross-Peterborough Signalling Panel Boundary
Sandy
To Cambridge
Biggleswade
Plasmor
Arlesey
To Bedford
Three Counties
Cambridge Jcn
To Cambridge
Hitchin
Stevenage
Stevenage
Langley water troughs
Redland
Langley Jcns
To Hertford N

Knebworth and Stevenage

KNEBWORTH: Gresley 'A3' 'Pacific' No 60065 *Knight of Thistle* was one of the first batch of 4-6-2s to be built by the North British Locomotive Works to supplement the LNER's Doncaster build. This was in August 1924, the locomotive being reclassified 'A1' to 'A3' following a 1947 rebuild. In this photograph 60065, with smoke deflectors and a double chimney, works an up express through Knebworth in 1963.

With the same road bridge in the background but the trackwork reduced to four plain tracks, the southbound 'Flying Scotsman' is seen in the second view on 30 May 1968 with Class 55 'Deltic' No 9003 *Meld* at its head.

By 15 October 1994 the scene has changed even more, with a number of multiple dwelling buildings constructed in the old goods siding area and the station platforms extended at the north end. The train is the 13.05 Leeds-King's Cross InterCity service with DVT No 82223 leading and power supplied from the rear by Class 91 No 91022 *Robert Adley*. *David Percival/BM*

LANGLEY JUNCTION: Although the idea of building the Hertford Loop as an alternative to quadrupling the main line obtained Parliamentary approval in 1898, another 20 years was to pass before it carried any through traffic. Even then the full route was to have a somewhat chequered history until it acquired electric services in 1977/8. During the summer of 1968 pairs of 'Baby Deltics' were rostered to work the evening coal empties from Palace Gates to Whitemoor. On this partic-ular day, 13 June, D5909 (in blue) and D5900 have passed beneath the main line and are climbing up the down side con-nection to join it.

The car park in the foreground, the overhead electric cur-rent supply equipment and the background factory make the scene appear more changed than it really is. The real change lies in the use of Class 317 EMUs on a route that once had a job to justify its LNER steam railcars. *David Percival/BM*

LANGLEY JUNCTION: The support operations for engineering work taking place at Langley Junction on 23 June 1968 are entirely dominated by BR Class 2 'Baby Deltics', four of them in fact. D5903 is out of picture ahead of the ballast wagons on the Up Slow line; D5904 stands in the foreground ahead of the bogie bolster wagons loaded with track sections; while behind the latter are D5901 and D5908, the former standing on the Down Slow line after bringing in the engineers' crane.

With catenary and support masts now festooning the area, and the foliage that has built up on the right precluding an exactly similar viewpoint, Class 317/2 No 317354 hurries the 13.02 Cambridge-King's Cross service between Stevenage and Langley Junction on 15 October 1994. The gasholder is still there to place the scene. *David Percival/BM*

STEVENAGE: BR's Type 4 'Peak' Class of locomotives were not normally seen at the front of the 'Flying Scotsman', although theoretically quite up to the task. Be that as it may, D176 is running half an hour late as it heads through Stevenage with the up service on 8 July 1967. This station, seen in the photograph in its traditional Great Northern style, was closed six years later on 23 July 1973 to be replaced by a more modern one located about a mile further south. The change resulted from the Stevenage New Town development and the desire to incorporate easily accessible rail facilities therein.

Passing the site of the original Stevenage station, DVT No 82221 leads the 07.00 Glasgow Central-King's Cross InterCity train, which is propelled from the rear by Class 91 No 91018 *Robert Louis Stevenson*. *David Percival/BM*

The era of 'Deltic'-hauled services on the East Coast Main Line gave way to that of the Class 254 High Speed Train sets. These were a 1977 10-car (two power units plus eight Mk III coaches) version of the nine-car Class 253 units, which had transformed the WR main lines out of Paddington. Here, in the original blue/grey livery, Class 254 set No 254027 enters Stevenage station with the 10.00 Edinburgh-King's Cross service on 5 April 1981. Class 43 power car No 43108 leads the train, one of several long-distance services to call at Stevenage to provide the outer-suburban area with access to direct, fast, through trains. *BM*

Hitchin to Offord

HITCHIN: *Above* Class 31/1 No 31118 hauls southbound empty Cartics through Hitchin station on 19 November 1986. In steam days the evening double-headed service for Cambridge/Peterborough used to divide at the down platform on the left. After running forward and allowing the train engine and Cambridge portion to depart, the Peterborough engine would then set back on to its vehicles. Meanwhile, in the way of knowing rail regulars everywhere, the latter's passengers would have made a carefully timed visit to the station refreshment rooms for a cup of tea! On the up side, behind the locomotive, is the site of Hitchin's old loco depot, a modest affair whose duties included providing power for the London-end engineer's sidings. *BM*

ARLESEY: *Right* At the time the InterCity sector was changing its livery many trains could be seen with both old and new colours. Providing a graphic example, even in black and white, the 07.18 Peterborough-King's Cross service passes Arlesey on 30 August 1988 powered by Class 89 No 89001, which is working with an InterCity 125 HST formation.

Along with neighbouring Three Counties, the original Arlesey station closed on 5 January 1959. It was a notorious bottleneck where four tracks became two, but this has all gone and there are now four tracks plus a modern station serving new housing developments. Unfortunately the signalmen's strike meant that there were no trains to be seen there on the evening of 8 September 1994. *Both BM*

BIGGLESWADE: In steam days the goods yard at Biggleswade would have been busy with produce from the market garden area of which the town is a centre. After carting, weighing, checking, loading, labelling and invoicing, the fitted vans would be attached to express freight services like 'The Five-Fifteen North Eastern' (see page 76) or 'The Six O'Clock West Riding' from King's Cross. Other loads would head south for early morning delivery to the Covent Garden, Spitalfields and Borough markets in London. On 7 May 1981 Biggleswade yard still has a role to play as a Class 31 pulls out with a southbound engineers' train.

Subsequently the area became a private rail-served facility, although the former GN goods shed has been demolished. The scene on 8 September 1994 also reveals a new platform canopy and abandonment of the old loading dock. *Both BM*

BIGGLESWADE: Entering Biggleswade station from the north on 7 May 1981, the 16.42 train from Huntingdon to Hitchin is formed of a Metro-Cammell Class 101 DMU that consists of cars Nos E51437 and E56382, both painted in off-white with blue body stripe.

The only changes in the second view are electrification and more lineside shrubbery. The former has vastly improved Biggleswade's service, catering for the constant northwards extension of the London commuter belt. In this picture, taken on 8 September 1994, Class 317/2 No 317372 leads an eight-car formation into the station on its journey from Peterborough to King's Cross, which it will accomplish in 57 minutes despite seven stops. *Both BM*

SANDY: Sandy used to be another bottleneck on the route north from King's Cross, the Down Slow section from Biggleswade ending under the wheels of Class 'A4' 'Pacific' No 60028 *Walter K. Whigham* in this photograph. Under clear signals the locomotive rushes a northbound express through the Bedfordshire junction in August 1960, making the most of this long, near-flat section of fertile agricultural land. The wagons in the goods yard appear to be cattle vans but, like Biggleswade, Sandy was noted for its market garden produce loadings and for the grain business of S. C. Banks.

The latter's silos can be seen in the second view, which also shows the reconstruction from two to four tracks using space formerly occupied on the left by the Cambridge–Bedford line. On the Down Fast on 13 August 1994 Class 91 No 91029 *Queen Elizabeth II* has charge of the 18.00 King's Cross–Edinburgh InterCity service. *John C. Baker/BM*

SANDY: Incorporating an early local venture known as Captain Peel's Railway, the section between Sandy and Potton having been originally opened in 1857 by Captain William Peel to link his estates with the GN main line, the former LNWR/LMS Cambridge-Sandy-Bedford-Bletchley route provided useful cross-country links and was, at one period, scheduled for development. However, it fell into

decline with withdrawal of the Cambridge-Bedford passenger services on 1 January 1968, but the subsequent lifting of track did at least permit the complete remodelling of the surviving, ex-GN/LNER, portion of the station. Here Sandy is seen in August 1960, before that process, with its flower beds in full bloom and with Stanier '5MT' 4-6-0 No 45331 heading for Cambridge with a coal train.

Class 317/1 EMU No 317307 makes the Sandy stop with the 19.02 service from Huntingdon to King's Cross on 13 August 1994. Although the same elevation is no longer available - at least not without being electrocuted - the background houses still link the two views, and the changes in the station are evident. *John C. Baker/BM*

SANDY: North of Sandy the former LMS line to Bedford became single track and continued that way almost to Bedford St Johns station. The bridge taking it across the East Coast Main Line is seen here on 1 January 1966 with a Cambridge-Oxford DMU.

At a point somewhat nearer Sandy on 8 September 1994 the secondary line has disappeared, leaving only its trackbed. The ex-LNER and ex-LMS routes were formerly linked by a wartime spur trailing into the former a little way ahead of the photographs. The 'sandhills' on the right here were once a Roman settlement. *G. Body/BM*

OFFORD: From Sandy the main line runs through the former station at Tempsford and on to St Neots. It is then joined by the River Ouse, the two being almost side by side between Little Paxton and Offord Cluny. This proximity produced curves in the railway necessitating speed restrictions, but these were eased under the Stage One round of improvements at the beginning of the 1970s. The proximity of railway and waterway shows well in this view of Class 91 No 91030 *Palace of Holyroodhouse* sweeping past with a northbound InterCity express from King's Cross on 20 August 1994. *Ken Brunt*

5.
HUNTINGDON AND PETERBOROUGH

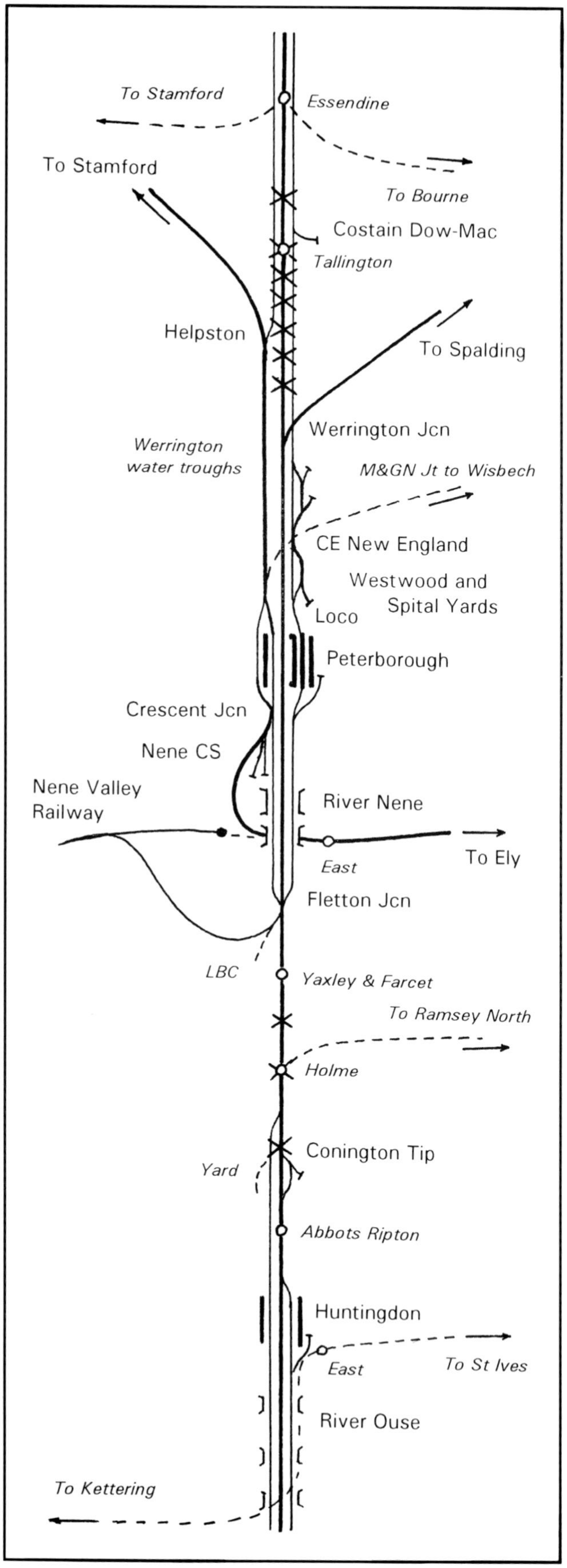

Brickfields dominate the landscape - and railway sidings - between Yaxley and Peterborough. From the 1912 GNR General Appendix.

Absolute.	57	58¾	Ouse box	1	49½	..	..	Midnight Saturday to Midnight Sunday	
	58	56	Huntingdon south junc.	..	77¼	..	..		
	58	57½	" south box	..	1½	..	..	Sundays, 8.0 a.m. to 6.0 a.m. Mondays	
	58	62½	Huntingdon joint station	..	4¾	..	..	See G.N. and G.E. joint line.	Huntingdon.
	58	69¾	Huntingdon station (Distance from south box)	..	12¾	..	..		
	59	2½	" north box	..	12½	Down	Up		
	61	7	Stukeley box ‡	2	4½	..	..	6.0 a.m. Sundays to 6.0 a.m. Mondays	
	62	1	Loys box (signals up lines only)	..	74	..	..	Midnight Saturday to Midnight Sunday	
	62	59	Abbott's Ripton crossing (No. 80)	..	58	..	..		
	63	39½	" " box	..	60½	Down	..		
	63	41½	Abbott's Ripton station	..	2½	..	..		Abbott's Ripton.
	65	45½	Wood Walton box	2	4	..	..	6.0 a.m. Sundays to 6.0 a.m. Mondays	
	67	29½	Connington box	1	63¾	..	..	Sundays 6.0 a.m. to Midnight	
	69	25¼	Holme box	1	75¼	Down	Up		
	69	26	Holme crossing (No. 87) *	..	0¾	..	..		
	69	29¼	Holme station and junction of Ramsey line	..	3¼	..	..		Holme.
	70	2	Holme lode crossing (No. 89)	..	52¾	..	..		
	71	6½	Stilton Fen box	1	4½	..	..	6.0 a.m. Sundays to 6.0 a.m. Mondays	Do.
	72	48½	Yaxley station	1	42½	..	..		
	72	52½	" box	..	4	Down	..	Sundays 3.45 a.m. to 12.30 p.m.; after passing of No. 128 down express to midnight.	Yaxley.
	72	58½	Norman Cross Brick Co.'s siding	..	5¾	..	..		
	73	4¼	Beeby's Brick siding	..	26½	..	..		
	73	19½	Yaxley Brick Co.'s siding	..	15	..	..		
	73	26¼	Fletton Crown Brick Co.'s siding	..	6½	..	..		
	73	39	Farcet Brick Co.'s siding	..	13¼	..	..		
	73	71	New Peterboro' Co.'s siding	..	32	..	..		Fletton.
	74	7½	Hicks Brick siding	..	16½	..	..		
	74	19¾	Plowman's Brick siding	..	12¼	..	..		
	74	76¼	Fletton Brick Co.'s siding	..	57	..	..		
			Fletton Brick Co.'s siding / London " " "	..	..	..	..		
	74	78	Fletton junction box	..	1¾	..	..	6.0 a.m. Sundays to 6.0 a.m. Mondays	Peterboro'.
	..	..	Hicks siding / London Brick Co.'s siding	..	..	..	..		Fletton.
	75	1½	Fletton goods station	..	3½	..	..		
	75	3½	" junction	..	2	..	..		Peterboro'.
	75	12	Farrow's Siding	..	8¾	..	..		Fletton.
	75	53½	Woodstone box (signals up lines only) ‡	..	41½	..	..	Midnight Saturday to Midnight Sunday	Peterboro'.
	76	16	Crescent junction	..	42½	..	..		
Down Main absolute, Up Main stop and caution.	76	16½	" " box	..	0½	..	..		Do.
	76	17	" crossing (No. 95) *	..	0¾	..	..		
	76	29	Peterboro' station	..	12	..	..		
	76	35	" north box	..	6	..	..		

Huntingdon area

SOUTH OF HUNTINGDON a couple of miles of level track precede a coming 3-mile rise at 1 in 200, and Gresley 'A3' 'Pacific' No 2578 *Bayardo* is pictured taking advantage of this to establish a good momentum for its heavy train. Built in 1924 as an 'A1' by the North British Locomotive Company, No 2578 was an early rebuild to 'A3' and worked in the latter form from 1928 to 1961.

In the modern view Class 91 No 91008 *Thomas Cook* works over the same stretch on 8 September 1994 in charge of the 15.00 King's Cross-Glasgow Central 'Scottish Pullman'. Below track level on the left is the course of the old Midland/LMS route from Kettering to Cambridge. *G. Body collection/BM*

HUNTINGDON: With a matching rake of InterCity Mk III stock, Class 43 power car No 43054 heads a King's Cross-bound HST through Huntingdon station during the summer of 1988. Despite modernised platforms and the trunk road overbridge, the up side buildings still proclaim the Great Northern ancestry of the station. Huntingdon East station, on the former Kettering to Cambridge line, was located in the station car park area on the right. It was the starting point of the Great Northern & Great Eastern Joint line route to Doncaster via March and Lincoln.

Mk IV stock forming the 10.05 Leeds-King's Cross express passing through Huntingdon station on 8 September 1994 is in the same position as the HST in 1988. Minor changes in the scene are the painting of the boundary fence, the erection of higher lighting masts and the lengthening of the up platform. *British Rail/BM*

HUNTINGDON: In the days when local services were still formed of blue-and-grey-liveried Class 101 DMUs, Peterborough-bound two-car Hitchin set No 23 calls at Huntingdon's down platform. Because of modest population levels and the pathing problems caused by track bottlenecks, the service on the Hitchin-Peterborough section was traditionally sparse. It was not a lot better when diesel multiple units replaced steam, but electrification combined with track and station improvements have now brought significant increases in trains and traffic.

On 8 September 1994 Class 317/1 EMU No 317318 calls at Huntingdon with the 12.38 train from King's Cross to Peterborough. The station lighting has been increased but the background trees are reduced in number. *British Rail/BM*

ABBOTS RIPTON: York-based Class 'V2' 2-6-2 No 60979 heads an up express from its home city in the summer of 1954. The location is the 1 in 200 down gradient from the site of Abbots Ripton station and Leys signal box. In better days lonely Abbots Ripton enjoyed a service of six trains each way, but by 1954 its users were few and far between and closure was only four years away. The location is also significant in rail-

way terms as the scene of a particularly nasty three-train accident in the winter snows of 1876.

At the same location on 13 August 1994 a Mk IV coaching rake is headed by DVT No 82203 and propelled by Class 91 No 91011 *Terence Cuneo*. Despite the lineside vegetation now evident the scene is fixed by the background bridge carrying the B road from the old station to Abbots Ripton village. *J. D. Mills/BM*

Holme Station. G.N.R.

HOLME: Conington, north of Abbots Ripton, used to be the site of a small wartime marshalling yard on the down side of the main line, and it still has an engineer's tip on the up. From there the main line runs straight and level, through the former Holme station. Stepping rather further back in time than other 'past' photographs, this view of Holme in Great Northern days is a reminder of the many wayside stations that the crack trains ignored and left to the humble and infrequent 'all-stations' services - 'parleys' as they were known to railwaymen. Holme also had a modest 5¾-mile branch east to Ramsey North, which survived a threat of omnibus replacement in the 1930s and struggled on until the LNER's own final year. Grain, potatoes and coal traffic then kept the branch open for freight for a few more years. *Lens of Sutton*

The line then runs on across a marshy area planted with silver birch trees and part of the Holme Fen nature reserve. Taking advantage of its easy passage across Denton Fen on 13 August 1994 Class 91 No 91021 makes a powerful picture as it hauls the 15.00 King's Cross-Glasgow Central express, the 'Scottish Pullman', at well over 100 mph. *BM*

Peterborough

YAXLEY: *Right* Passing the site of the erstwhile Yaxley & Farcet station on 13 August 1994, the 07.50 Inverness-King's Cross HST, the 'Highland Chieftain', is headed by Class 43 power car No 43108. Just south of the station, which closed from 6 April 1959, the East Coast Main Line has crossed Pig Water!

Seen through the bridge arch, the three brickyard chimneys are a reminder that both sides of the track hereabouts used to be dominated by brickmaking - pits, conveyors and kilns - all the way to Fletton. The industry thrived on near-self-combustible clay fired in the kilns of many small individual firms and later the London Brick Company, whose Phorpres trade name derived from the four pressings in the brick-making process. Conventional rail wagon haulage was bedevilled by shunting breakages but Freightliner schemes fared better. BR also carried pulverised fuel ash for claypit infilling. *BM*

Below The complexity of railway operations around Peterborough can be seen from this map taken from a District Engineer's diagram of 1950/51. *BR*

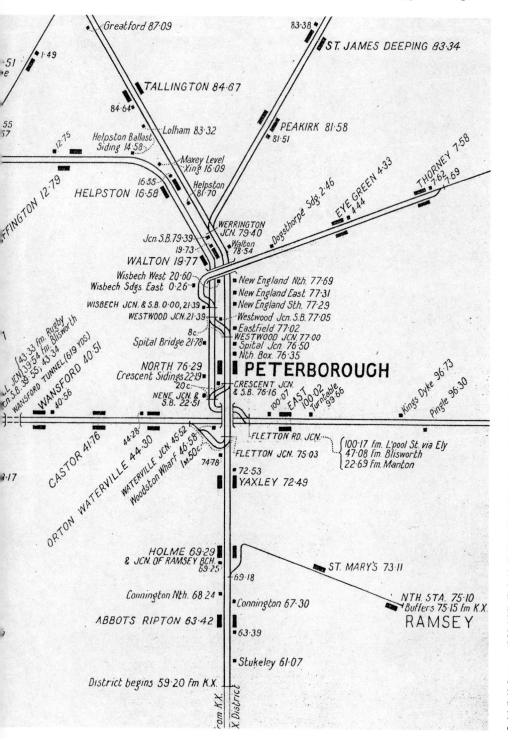

NENE VALLEY RAILWAY: *Right* The first rail access to Peterborough was in 1845 from Northampton on the London & Birmingham Railway's Blisworth branch, this later being joined by another route from Rugby. The two joined at Yarwell Junction, west of Wansford, which was also the junction for a long-closed GN branch from Stamford. After closure to passengers, then losing its residual mineral traffic, the section from Wansford to Peterborough was rescued by the Peterborough Railway Society. Now called the Nene Valley Railway the route runs through the recreational Nene Park to a station near the old LNWR Woodston Wharf and operates continental locomotives and stock among its many preservation activities. A physical connection with BR exists via Longueville and Fletton junctions, a line formerly used to serve the BSC sugar beet factory.

Having been formally named *Nene Valley Railway* at a ceremony on 23 March 1994 Class 31/5 No 31558 departs from Orton Mere station with a special train for Wansford. Manor Class 4-6-0 No 7819 *Hinton Manor* is also in attendance. *BM*

PETERBOROUGH: *Above and left* English Electric Type 4 (later Class 40) D350 is seen approaching Peterborough North station on 27 October 1962 hauling a King's Cross-York express. Crescent Junction signal box on the right controlled the link between the main line and the route up from Peterborough East. The original Peterborough North goods depot is on the left of the picture, while straight ahead lay Nene Sidings. Coaches stabled there on a cold winter's night were like travelling refrigerators to those catching early morning services, the steam heating frequently losing its battle with the riverside chill.

The second view graphically depicts the south end remodelling at Peterborough. The main features of this were a new down island platform and through lines between this and the modified up-side facilities. On 13 August 1994 the 10.40 King's Cross-Edinburgh service, led by Class 91 No 91013 *Michael Faraday*, is leaving the Down Fast for No 4 Platform Line. The Down Slow can be seen crossing to the right to unite with the ex-MR Stamford line as far as Helpston. *Philip H. Wells/BM*

Left Like a great many others of its kind, Crescent Bridge at Peterborough replaced a level crossing, although it is hard to visualise such a thing in the light of today's trains and speeds. This view, looking from the other side of the bridge but in the same direction as the previous two, amplifies the remodelling changes at Peterborough with the route of the original platform lines on the left, the through lines in the centre and the platform and Stamford lines beyond. On the Down Fast line Class 58 No 58040 *Cottam Power Station* is at the head of a good load of northbound CSA Presflos on 13 August 1994. *BM*

PETERBOROUGH: Approaching from the north with an express for King's Cross, Class 'A4' 'Pacific' No 60006 *Sir Ralph Wedgwood* has shut off steam for the Peterborough stop on 24 May 1959. Peterborough, like other railway centres, was littered with railway buildings devoted to every conceivable purpose. The Great Northern Hotel outside the station had its own bread ovens in one of these, while on the other side of the tracks stood the LMS coaling tower.

Apart from a line-up of stabled civil engineers' Class 31s, today's country-end approaches to Peterborough now look rather bland, although some of the old buildings on the right have managed to survive. On 12 August 1994 an InterCity 225 Mk IV set comes off the main line into the platform road to make the scheduled stop of the 11.05 from Leeds to King's Cross. DVT No 82204 leads with Class 91 No 91023 providing traction from the rear. *Both BM*

PETERBOROUGH NEW ENGLAND SHED: Inside the repair shops of New England shed (35A) on 24 May 1959, attention is being given to an assorted collection of engines, several of which have dropped driving wheels. Among the machines receiving attention are Class 'A5/1' 4-6-2T No 69827, Class 'A4' No 60008 *Dwight D. Eisenhower* and Class 'A3' No 60082 *Neil Gow*. There are springs, tools and all sorts of other things lying around, while the two fitters beside *Neil Gow* enjoy their 'snap' (meal).

From the same position today nothing of the New England shed complex can be seen, the site now forming a large and modern Parcel Force depot. *Both BM*

HELPSTON: For the 5 miles from Peterborough, past the up side remains of New England yard then Werrington Junction, where the Spalding line departs, the East Coast Main Line is accompanied by the ex-MR Stamford line and uses the latter's down track as a Down Slow. All this ends at Helpston where the Stamford route veers off north-west and the ECML again becomes a conventional set of four tracks. There are seven crossings between New England and Tallington, that at Helpston seen here on 30 August 1989 being approached by Class 56 56078 with a northbound train of EEC Quarries hoppers. The attractive but tiny crossing-keeper's cottage is still there but not the footbridge from which this photograph was taken. *BM*

North to Essendine

TALLINGTON: The Great Northern Railway's first big commercial success, the one that finally brought a smile to the faces of the long-suffering shareholders, was securing the movement of South Yorkshire coal to London, and for over 100 years wagonload coal traffic was then to be a familiar sight on the East Coast Main Line, standing in the yards at Doncaster, New England or Ferme Park or on the move as in this photograph taken near Tallington on 10 July 1960. Heading the train is Class '02/2' 2-8-0 No 63939, a representative of a design that originated with the GNR in 1921 and went on to become one of the LNER standard classes. A total of 66 of these heavy goods engines was built.

In the same place but moving about 100 mph faster, the 07.50 Inverness-King's Cross HST, the 'Highland Chieftain', races south on 27 August 1994, Class 43 power car No 43039 leading. *Philip H. Wells/BM*

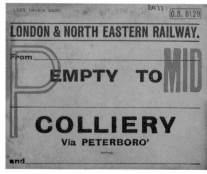

LONDON & NORTH EASTERN RAILWAY.

From EMPTY TO MID COLLIERY
Via PETERBORO'

O.S. 8120

ESSENDINE: Work-stained 'A3' Class 'Pacific' No 60047 *Donovan* approaches Essendine on 16 July 1960 hauling a King's Cross-Edinburgh express. *Donovan* was one of the 1924 'A1s' rebuilt as Class 'A3' in the first month of nationalisation, then given a double chimney in July 1959. In the light of the engine's appearance one is bound to wonder what it made of the 12-mile climb that lay ahead.

On 27 August 1994 Class 91 No 91029 *Queen Elizabeth II* and the 15.00 King's Cross-Glasgow Central 'Scottish Pullman' will make light of the rising road. *Philip H. Wells/BM*

ESSENDINE: Another photograph taken on the same stretch south of Essendine pictures a King's Cross-Newcastle express on 15 August 1957. The locomotive is the Gresley 'Pacific' No 60113 *Great Northern* in its little-loved Thompson rebuild form. This was the first of the LNER's 'A1' 4-6-2 express passenger engines and went on proud exhibition at King's Cross in April 1922, straight from Doncaster Works. Evoking less pleasure was the rebuild by Edward Thompson in 1945, but some of the worst excesses of that process, including the ludicrously shortened cab sides, were quickly put right and the locomotive appears here in its final Class 'A1/1' form.

There can be little complaint about the appearance of the InterCity 225 in the second view. The train is the 15.10 service from King's Cross to Leeds on 27 August 1994 with Class 91 No 91025 *BBC Radio 1 FM* at its head. *Philip H. Wells/Ken Brunt*

ESSENDINE: *Opposite page* Until its closure from 15 June 1959 Essendine was a rural main-line junction. The 1856 branch from the outer face of the down island platform went to Stamford where the terminus was built in the same style as Burghley House, home of the line's sponsor, the Marquis of Exeter. From the up bay at Essendine a second branch was opened in 1860 to Bourne.

Today some of the Essendine buildings still survive, including the station master's substantial house. They preserve a Great Northern touch in a location that elsewhere is a picture of clean, fast track and straightforward overhead equipment. Making the most of this on 27 August 1994 is the 13.00 King's Cross-Glasgow Central InterCity 225 service powered by Class 91 91005 *Royal Air Force Regiment*. *G. Body/BM*

6.
GRANTHAM
AND
NEWARK

The lines around Barkston and Grantham and down Stoke Bank towards Essendine will always be associated with *Mallard*'s epic speed record run of 3 July 1938, remembered in this 1939 advertisement from the makers of the locomotive's blastpipe.

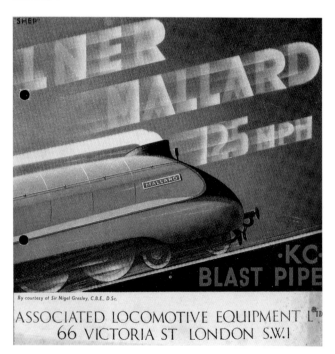

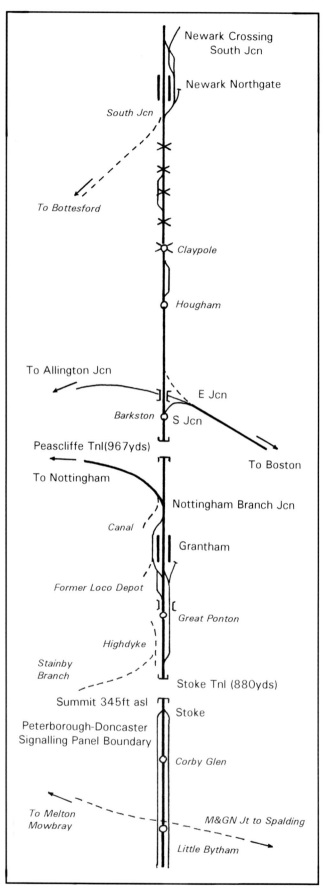

Stoke Bank

LITTLE BYTHAM: When this photograph was taken on 14 September 1965 Little Bytham station had been closed for passengers for six years, and its freight facilities were to end six weeks later. No doubt that explains the closed doors of the goods shed and the absence of wagons in the yard. Meanwhile Type 4 1Co-Co1 (later Class 40) D351 passes down the 1 in 200 of the lower part of Stoke Bank with a southbound express made up of maroon-liveried stock. Behind is a train of empty coal wagons being hauled in the same direction (although one wonders why) by Type 2 Bo-Bo (later Class 25) No D5195.

Little Bytham goods shed has a new lease of life in the second view, taken on 17 August 1994. The train is the 12.00 'Flying Scotsman' from Glasgow Central to King's Cross with Mk IV DVT No 82215 leading and Class 91 No 91027 providing power from the rear. The higher ground in the distance marks the area where the Midland line from Saxby crossed the ECML and became the M&GN Joint line. *Philip H. Wells/BM*

CORBY GLEN: The scenery pictured is typical of this rich agricultural part of Lincolnshire, and makes a marked contrast with the sleek trains and immaculate permanent way of the East Coast Main Line, especially on this section near Corby Glen, so well known for its role in the annals of high-speed rail traction. Three miles of a descending gradient of 1 in 178 lead from Stoke Tunnel to Corby Glen and have primed many an exciting run, which went largely unobserved except by the farming community. Moving at speed near Corby Glen on 8 September 1994, the 07.00 Glasgow Central-King's Cross InterCity 225 service is propelled by Class 91 No 91018 *Robert Louis Stevenson*, with Mk IV DVT No 82224 leading. *BM*

STOKE TUNNEL: The lineside vegetation in this picture of the north portal of Stoke Tunnel has now grown so much that a comparative photograph from the same position is just impossible. Yet no book about the East Coast Main Line could omit the inclusion of such an important location, where generations of northbound enginemen have breathed a sigh of relief and their southbound counterparts have experienced an instinctive moment of anticipation - even if only of a respite from shovel-work! The summit of the long climb from the south was Stoke Box, 100 miles from King's Cross and 354 feet above sea level, with the tunnel following at the top of the 5-mile descent at 1 in 200 to Grantham. Bursting from the 880 yards of tunnel on 24 May 1980 is the 09.35 King's Cross-Newcastle HST, formed of set No 254032 and headed by Class 43 power car No 43133. *BM*

STOKE TUNNEL: Hauling a light mixed southbound freight, Class 37/0 No 37006 approaches the tunnel on 24 May 1980. The open area on the left marks Highdyke Junction, from which the GNR opened mineral lines west to Sproxton and Stainby. Empties went thence to the iron ore workings, and returning loaded traffic assembled there for onward movement north.

Propelled from the rear by Res Class 90/0 No 90020 *Colonel Bill Cockburn CBE TD*, the 16.40 InterCity service from Leeds to King's Cross is headed by a Mk IV DVT as it climbs towards Stoke Tunnel on 27 August 1994. Electrification has resulted in the tree on the right being cut back and the colour light signals being relocated out of view to the right. *Both BM*

Grantham

GRANTHAM: This Lincolnshire market town was an important stopping point for coaches on the old Great North Road and for engine changes on the railway main line in the steam era. Grantham shed (later 34F) stood on the left of the first picture, which was taken from the London end of the complex on 24 May 1980. In it Class 40 No 40117 begins the climb to Stoke summit at the head of nine coaches forming the 08.05 York to King's Cross.

A plethora of overhead catenary and support masts now completely obliterates Grantham station from the same viewpoint, and foliage on the right prevents an exact angle being used. On 7 September 1994 Class 46/7 No 47676 *Northamptonshire* heads south with an Inspection Saloon past a track layout much simplified compared with 14 years earlier. The Aveling-Barford factory on the right has been demolished, emptying the area traditionally occupied by Grantham's heavy industry. *Both BM*

GRANTHAM: A BR Derby Class 114 DMU consisting of cars Nos 56014 and 56003 stands at Grantham on 25 September 1976 forming the 14.06 local service to Nottingham. That line originated as part of a grand scheme to link Manchester with the port of Boston, which also embodied Grantham's second branch, the line east through Sleaford. A third service also used to depart from the country end of the down island platform at Grantham, that to Lincoln via Honington, but this ended on 1 November 1965.

In addition to simplifcation of the track layout at Grantham, the station itself was also modernised in the 1980s. This shows in a comparison of the platform canopy, which remains traditional although now much less elaborate. Over the years various permutations of cross-country service have called at Grantham, the picture taken on 7 September 1994 showing one of Regional Railways' North West-East Anglia workings in the shape of the 06.48 Liverpool Lime Street to Great Yarmouth formed of Class 158/0 No 158794. *Both BM*

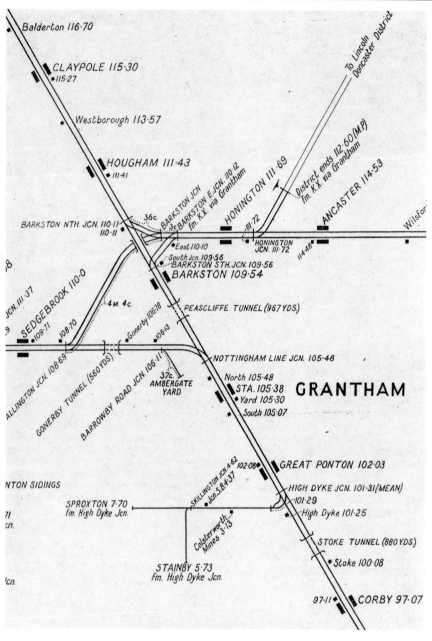

Railways around Grantham and Barkston, from a map based on a District Engineer's diagram of 1950/51. *BR*

BARKSTON: Passing Barkston South Junction at speed on 6 August 1994, Mk IV DVT No 82210 leads the 08.00 Glasgow Central-King's Cross express with a Class 91, out of sight, providing traction from the rear in accordance with the standard pattern of ECML working. Barkston used to have its own station at this point until it lost its trains from 16 March 1955, but the location is better remembered as the place at which *Mallard* turned its train before embarking upon the run that produced the 126 mph world record for steam traction. After arriving from London the down train ran from Barkston South Junction to Barkston East, where the Sleaford/Boston line is joined by that from Allington Junction on the Nottingham branch, and then reversed back to the main line over the now-abandoned spur to Barkston North. *Ken Brunt*

Newark,
Great Northern Railway Station.

Newark

NEWARK is served by two railway routes, that of the East Coast Main Line and the lesser, but still important, ex-Midland Railway line from Nottingham to Lincoln. Newark's two separate stations are known, respectively, as Northgate and Castle, the 'past' view here giving a good impression of Northgate in Great Northern days. The sheer volume of signs and posters is amazing, but those were the days when each platform had its Ladies, Gents and General waiting rooms, not to mention Left Luggage, Refreshment Room, Telegraph Office and other such places that had to be labelled.

With the Potts station clock and a little of the old down-side canopy still in place, modern Newark is a much simpler, better-lit station and is also an hour 'nearer' to King's Cross! On 8 September 1994 the 06.00 Edinburgh to King's Cross service sweeps through the station with the driver in Mk IV DVT No 82228 and Class 91 No 91011 *Terence Cuneo* pushing from the rear. *Lens of Sutton/BM*

NEWARK: Another example of the short-lived experimental DMU livery of the middle 1970s. In off-white with blue stripe, a Class 114 twin formed of cars Nos E50040 and E56022 sets out from Newark Northgate station on 6 September 1980. The train is the 16.03 to Cleethorpes. In pre-BR days Newark Northgate had trains along the main line and to Nottingham via Bottesford, but the service east to Lincoln was provided from Castle station on the ex-LMS line. However, with the end of the Grantham-Lincoln service and the wholesale clo-sures in East Lincolnshire, the route from London to Lincoln and beyond became via Newark and the spur this DMU is using.

Powering through Newark Northgate on 8 September 1994, Class 91 No 91017 *Commonwealth Institute* heads the 09.00 King's Cross-Edinburgh InterCity 225 service. There is now a car park where the goods shed stood, the up sidings appear abandoned and the station footbridge has been relocated. *Both BM*

NEWARK: On 6 September 1980 Brush Class 47/4 No 47457 heads an up train of Mk I stock - probably an 'Awayday' special - over the section between the Nottingham-Lincoln line and Newark Northgate station. Behind the train runs the link to the single line connection between the two routes, which runs 11 chains from Newark Crossing South to East junctions. In the second view the vegetation has grown so much that the houses seem to have become bungalows! The background road has been improved and the railway has acquired all the trappings of electrification.

Putting these to good use on 18 September 1994 is the 09.05 from Leeds to King's Cross with DVT No 82220 at the front and Class 91 No 91030 *Palace of Holyroodhouse* at the rear. *Both BM*

7.
TRENT TO DON

The grand up-side buildings at Retford carry this rather unusual plaque. *G. Body*

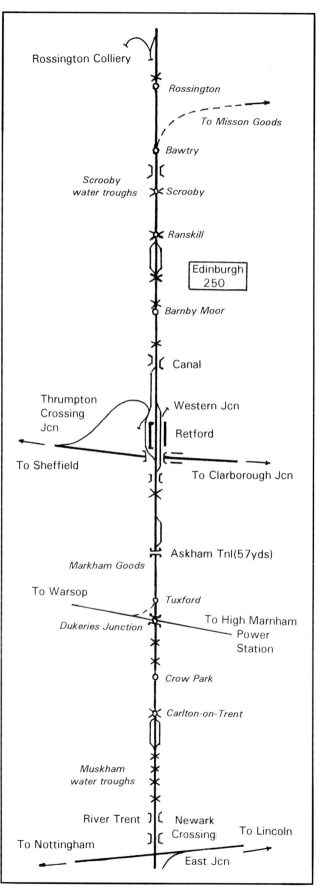

North of Newark

NEWARK: The East Coast Main Line used to have 'flat' crossings at Newark, Retford and Darlington, but only that at Newark survives. Such a crossing really represents no greater complication than a junction would; indeed, the section blocked by the crossing train will tend to clear more quickly, although it still has a limiting effect on the paths available on the busy main line. This scene on 23 March 1991 shows the 16.20 Leeds-King's Cross service, which has passed over the bridge across the River Trent and then the Nottingham-Lincoln line and is heading for Newark station. A Mk IV DVT leads and Class 91 No 91011 propels.

Also on 23 March 1991 we see Class 150/1 'Sprinter' No 150138 crossing the ECML with the 17.05 service from Newark Castle to Lincoln. This vantage point gives a good view of the Trent bridge. *Both BM*

CROW PARK: North of Newark the East Coast Main Line follows the direction of the River Trent, through a number of crossings, to the site of the old station at Carlton-on-Trent. This closed to passengers on 2 March 1953, followed by its neighbour Crow Park on 6 October 1958. Crow Park station also used to serve the village of Normanton-on-Trent, the nearest community to the scene pictured in this photograph of Peppercorn Class 'A1' 'Pacific' No 60123 *H. A. Ivatt* at the head of a King's Cross-Leeds/Bradford express on 24 May 1959. Built at Doncaster in 1949, 60123 was named in the following year, but then lasted only until 1962.

Local stations on the two-track section north of Grantham never got much of a service because of the demands of through trains. Their prospects would have been no better in the present electric age, represented by the 12.10 King's Cross to Leeds on 7 September 1994. Class 91 No 91022 *Robert Adley* speeds through a countryside little changed except that the cows have given way to sheep. At least the latter are in no danger from a spark-induced fire despite the extra foliage. *Both BM*

TUXFORD: The road ahead is clear for a southbound express passing Tuxford North station on 24 May 1959 and hauled by Doncaster (36A)-allocated Gresley 'A3' Class 'Pacific' No 60066 *Merry Hampton*. Until four years earlier Tuxford had also had a station on the ex-LD&EC line from Chesterfield Market Place to Lincoln. Surviving after passenger closure to serve High Marnham power station, this crossed the main line ahead of *Merry Hampton* at Dukeries Junction where the two-level station closed in 1950. In the right foreground of this picture is an excellent example of the then modern semaphore signal with concrete posts. The 'on' arm controls access to the spur leading round to Tuxford Central.

Passing the site of the old Tuxford North station on 7 September 1994, the DVT-led 08.00 Glasgow Central-King's Cross InterCity 225 service has the usual Class 91 rear-end power, in this case provided by No 91002 *Durham Cathedral*. Although the station and surrounding buildings have gone, the chimneys of the house in the top right-hand corner are still apparent behind the trees. *Both BM*

ASKHAM: On 8 September 1957 an Edinburgh-King's Cross express is pictured near Askham Tunnel, south of Retford, with Class 'A4' 'Pacific' No 60028 *Walter K. Whigham* in charge. Formerly flanked by Markham and Gamston signal boxes, the modest 57-yard tunnel tops a minor summit between Crow Park and Retford.

Its 3 miles at 1 in 178/200 will not have made much impression on the progress of the 07.55 Aberdeen-King's Cross HST pictured on 7 September 1994 with Class 43 InterCity 125 power car No 43107 about to enter the northern portal of the tunnel. *Eric Oldham/BM*

Heading north from Askham Tunnel on 7 September 1994 Class 56 No 56074 *Kellingley Colliery* hauls a train of empty steel bolster wagons. The locomotive has been given the new black and orange colours of Loadhaul Freight but has yet to receive the 'Loadhaul' insignia on the body sides. *BM*

Retford

RETFORD: The 12.05 departure from King's Cross for Hull pulls away from the Retford stop on 6 September 1980, powered by Type 5 'Deltic' No 55014 *The Duke of Wellington's Regiment*. Over half the class carried military names, the rest those of notable racehorses, continuing a tradition dating back to the last century. Not that the 'Deltics' would uphold this particular tradition much longer for their withdrawal had already begun when this picture was taken.

Passing Retford at speed in the second photograph on 7 September 1994, Class 91 91015 leads the 14.10 King's Cross-Leeds service. On the Down Slow line at the end of the platform can be seen the connection to the engineers' depot and the departure point of the mile-long single line round to Thrumpton Crossing Junction on the Sheffield route. *Both BM*

RETFORD: Before the days of the Great Central Railway and its London Extension, the Great Northern ran an excellent service over its main line from King's Cross and on to Sheffield via Worksop. In those days the Sheffield-Lincoln/Cleethorpes line crossed the East Coast Main Line on the level to the south of the station, but reconstruction in more recent times has routed the secondary line through an underpass and thus done away with the former 60 mph speed limitation. Reconstruction at Retford has also meant that calling northbound trains use the outer face of the former down island. The 15.10 King's Cross to Leeds is doing just that on 7 September 1994 when its rolls into Retford headed by the last Class 91 to be built, No 91031 *Sir Henry Royce*. *BM*

Class 58 No 58041 *Ratcliffe Power Station* passes through Retford station on 7 September 1994 hauling northbound PAA hoppers. The main station buildings along the up side are very impressive although now much larger than the station activity warrants. *BM*

RETFORD: In the original InterCity blue/grey livery, the up 'Flying Scotsman' HST approaches Retford on 6 September 1980. The Class 254 sets built for the East Coast Main Line consisted of two 1st Class and six Standard Class vehicles, as in this case where set No 254023 is headed by power car No 43101.

At the same location on 7 September 1994 the longer nine-coach formation of today's InterCity 225 services is apparent. The train is the 15.35 Doncaster to King's Cross, consisting of leading DVT, standard Mk IV coaching set and trailing Class 91 No 91027. *Both BM*

8.
DONCASTER

Doncaster - an extract from *On Either Side*, an LNER East Coast Main Line publication from the 1920s.

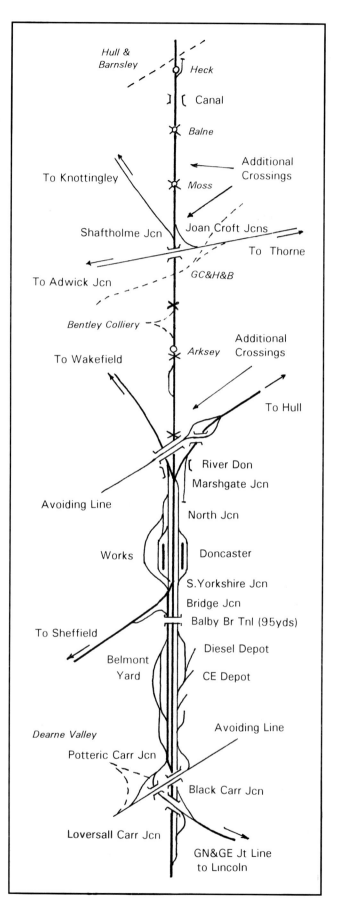

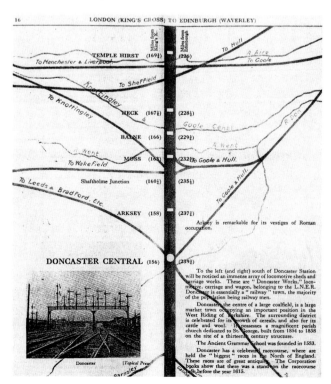

Southern approaches

BRIDGE JUNCTION: Apart from a minor 1 in 198 'pimple' the ECML section between Retford and Doncaster is nearly level. Along this stretch there used to be stations at Barnby Moor, Ranskill, Scrooby, Bawtry and Rossington, but only a few level crossings and emergency crossings preserve their whereabouts, although the colliery connection at Rossington is extant. Much has also changed within the once huge railway complex south of Doncaster. In the 'past' photograph York (50A)-allocated 'V2' class 2-6-2 No 60982 is seen heading south from Doncaster with a long Newcastle-King's Cross express on 31 August 1954. The location appears to be Bridge Junction where the Decoy yard complex commenced.

Although the houses in the background remain, the second illustration shows a typical reduction in trackwork. The scene was photographed again on 28 August 1994 and captured the 10.00 InterCity 225 service from Edinburgh to King's Cross led by DVT No 82201 and propelled by Class 91 No 91208 *Guide Dog*. *Both BM*

DONCASTER YARD: In a thoroughly grimy condition Class 'B16/2' 4-6-0 No 61421 stands at the head of an unfitted Class H freight 'waiting for the road' to the south. In the background is Doncaster engine shed (36A), while the signal gantry in the foreground provides an interesting example of the separation of signal wires and counterweighting of signals. The date is 31 August 1954.

Now governed by 'colour lights', the same freight line skirts the present-day Doncaster MPD, but the sidings between the depot and the running line have been lifted and the encroachment of nature is much in evidence. In the changes south of Doncaster, Up and Down Decoy Yards and the Up and Down Mineral Yards were slimmed down to provide a smaller upside complex for engineers' stock, a Down Decoy yard for defective wagons and a new Belmont facility for Speedlink traffic. *Both BM*

One of the most significant dividends from expanding electrification has been the increasing capability to erect masts and perform other construction work at truly remarkable speed. This has been partly attributable to mounting drilling and other equipment on rail wagons and carrying out several operations simultaneously. Here an electrification train formed of concrete mixers mounted on bogie wagons passes through Doncaster on 17 November 1988. At its head is Class 31/4 No 31441, still in BR 'Corporate blue' livery. *BM*

DONCASTER SHED: Thompson's 1942 'B1' Class of 4-6-0 mixed traffic engines was eventually to number over 400. The first 40 carried the names of wild animals and a few of the later engines were named after notable people, in the case of No 61250 pictured here, *A. Harold Bibby*. The photograph was taken outside the locomotive's home shed at Doncaster on 31 August 1954 and the locomotive looks good enough to tackle any of the very varied diagrams allocated to this depot.

Despite the loss of a great many sidings consequent upon the change from wagonload to trainload freight Doncaster remains a busy rail centre as this present-day scene testifies. The old Doncaster shed frontage would have been where the crossing is now situated, but that part of the building has been demolished. In the 'B1's' 1954 position on 28 August 1994 is Class '08' shunter No 08581 *Imogen*. The Class 37, 47 and 56 locomotives would have been inside the old building. *Both BM*

Doncaster station

DONCASTER: Stepping further back in time than usual the photograph of the London end of Doncaster station in Great Northern days shows just how extensive are the changes time has wrought. Who now remembers Shakespeare signal box, the old up-side end-dock or the sidings in front of 'The Plant' being so full? Only the footbridge access to the Works seems to have survived without significant alteration.

In the 'present' view the same southern approaches to Doncaster are pictured on 28 August 1994 with the noon King's Cross departure to Glasgow Central on the Fast line, powered by Class 91 No 91015. The bridge from which the photographs were taken was the scene of a 1951 derailment accident in which 14 people were killed.
Lens of Sutton/BM

DONCASTER: Spotters to the left of us, spotters to the right of us. . . On a typical summer Saturday at Doncaster in the 1950s, holding centre stage in the photograph is Class 'B16/3' 4-6-0 No 61464 coasting into the station on 23 May 1959 with an express for Hull. Stock to the right includes a double-cylinder gas tank, while 'perishable' vans are being shunted past the goods depot, itself full of box vans.

With a Class 142 'Pacer' in the Doncaster bay platform forming a local service to Sheffield, the centrepiece of the more recent view is an InterCity Cross Country HST. The service is the 10.43 Bristol Temple Meads to York with Class 43 power car No 43029 leading. Quite a lot has changed in 15 years, including the bridge from which the previous photographs were taken. Doncaster's up platform has been lengthened using space vacated by access lines to the old goods depot and much of the down-side trackwork has gone, matching the reduction in activity in the former Works. There are no spotters to be seen and the church is sandwiched between a tower block and the Doncaster panel building. *Both BM*

DONCASTER: These high-level views of Doncaster station were taken from the overlooking car park on 31 January 1981 and 28 August 1994 respectively. The background in both cases is made up of the buildings of Doncaster Works where so many noteworthy locomotive designs were conceived and fabricated. In the earlier photograph HST set No 254014 stands at the main down platform with the 10.05 King's Cross-Edinburgh service. Alongside are DMUs providing connecting services, while in the background Class 31/1 No 31119 is pass-

ing through with a load of northbound British Industrial Sand hoppers.

In the second view the Class 158 in the up platform is a Regional Railways North East service from Cleethorpes to Manchester Piccadilly. At the northbound local platforms is a Class 321/9 on a Leeds service and a number of 'Pacers' wait for their next duty. Despite the disappearance of the tracks in the foreground beneath a car park extension the same coach is still there, looking rather the worse for wear! *Both BM*

DONCASTER: Departing from Doncaster 'Sandringham' Class 'B17/6' No 61643 *Champion Lodge* makes a full-blooded start with the 09.07 local service to Peterborough on 31 August 1954. *Champion Lodge* was a March engine that had probably worked one of the many March/Whitemoor to Doncaster duties over the GN&GE Joint line via Lincoln. Note the sharp curve on the access to the back roads of the goods depot and the water crane with its attendant brazier.

With the up platform now lengthened, Mk IV DVT No 82206 enters Doncaster in the same position but heading the 13.00 service from Edinburgh to King's Cross. In this case the almost inevitable Class 91 is not providing propulsion, the motive power being Class 90 No 90021. *Both BM*

MARSHGATE JUNCTION, just north of Doncaster station, is the point at which the East Coast Main Line parts company with the lines to Hull and Wakefield. Here, on 31 August 1954, Robinson Class 'J11' 0-6-0 No 64404 trundles into Doncaster with a Sheffield-bound freight working. The first examples of the 'J11' Class were built as far back as 1901 by the Great Central Railway. They were a familiar sight in the Doncaster area because of its extensive GCR connections.

The wires for Doncaster's public transport have gone from the bridge, but the railway below now has them in profusion. On 28 August 1994 Class 37/7 No 37886 passes beneath the same bridge with southbound steel wagons. Behind this the railway crosses the River Don from which Doncaster takes its name. *Both BM*

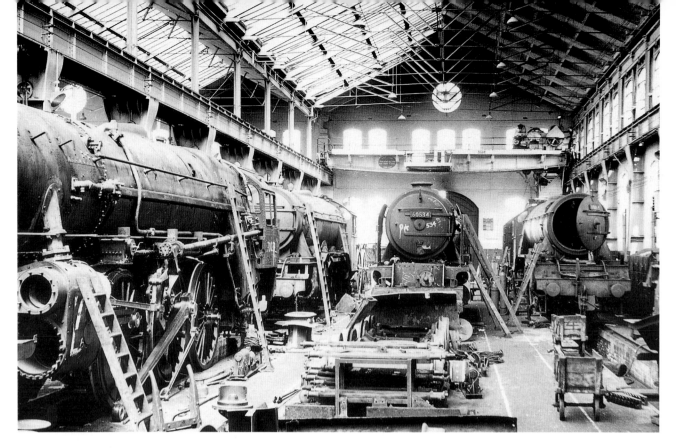

Doncaster Works

DONCASTER WORKS: Inside the Works on 23 May 1959 the scene appears one of great confusion with locomotives lifted off their leading wheels and others with their driving gear in apparently meaningless disarray. But this was all part of the rich panoply of 'shopping programmes' for heavy locomotive repairs, with the 'victims' in this case being BR Standard '7MT' Class 'Pacific' No 70039 *Sir Christopher Wren*, Class 'A3' 'Pacifics' Nos 60107 *Royal Lancer* and 60064 *Tagalie*, and Class 'A2' 'Pacific' No 60534 *Irish Elegance*.

By comparison the diesel era scene in the works on 19 August 1979 seems quite orderly, partly because the removable parts are larger. The three machines present are Class 55 No 55012 *Crepello*, Class 37 No 37232 and Class 50 No 50006 *Neptune*. *Both BM*

DONCASTER WORKS: *Top right* By the time of its first trial run on 12 December 1929 Gresley's experimental 4-6-4 locomotive had become known as 'Hush Hush' because of the secrecy surrounding its construction at Darlington Works. The combination of high-pressure water-tube boiler and four-cylinder compounding failed to work in practice and Class 'W1' No 10000 was rebuilt to more conventional three-cylinder form in 1937.

After spending the whole of its working life on the East Coast Main Line, proving a powerful but not particularly fast engine, the 4-6-4 was formally withdrawn in June 1959. Carrying the BR number 60700, the unique locomotive is pictured awaiting its fate in Doncaster Works yard on 23 May 1959. *BM*

Middle and bottom right These two photographs represent an activity rather than a location 'past and present'. In fact they are not very far apart in time, but one depicts the building process of a new class and the other the ignominious fate of an old one.

The first 30 locomotives of the 1976 Class 56 build came from Romania, with No 56031 and onwards being constructed by BREL. The scene at Doncaster Works on 19 August 1979 shows No 56066 a little further down the road to completion than 56070, which still has lifting lugs on its body shell. A sadder scene is that photographed in the works cutting yard on 10 August 1980 when the very mixed debris included both cabs from No 31005. *Both BM*

9.
SELBY
AND YORK

The Big Switch - a 1983 booklet giving alterations to train services during the change-over from the original main line to the new Selby Coalfield Diversion route.

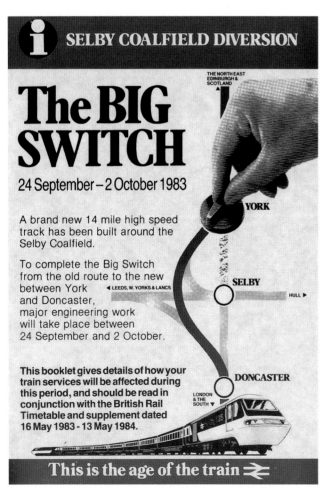

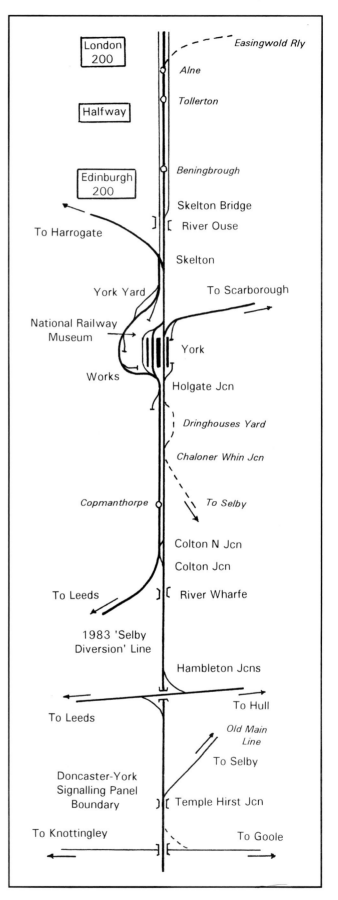

Selby

SELBY: A great change in the profile of the East Coast Main Line came into operation in 1983 when trains began running over 14 miles of new route between Doncaster and York. The old route of the main line through Selby and on to Chaloner Whin, the junction with the Leeds-York line, lay astride a massive area of high-quality coal deposits. The options of leaving a wide corridor beneath the railway unexploited or reducing speeds to minimise the risk of mining subsidence were both unacceptable and the decision was taken to build a new railway and abandon the old one north of Selby. The new line, which began at Temple Hirst Junction and ended at Colton Junction, was built for high-speed running using the most up-to-date permanent way techniques.

On 22 May 1959 'A4' Class 'Pacific' No 60025 *Falcon* approaches Selby via the original route with the northbound afternoon 'Talisman' express from King's Cross to Edinburgh. At Selby the East Coast Main Line used a section of the pioneer Leeds-Hull route through the station and across the swing-bridge over the River Ouse. This made the location important for transfers between the two lines, which explains the sizeable number of wagons in the sidings on the right of this picture.

The present day scene at the same location is one of stark contrast with no sidings and no trains. The once proud main line can now hardly be called even a local line as services on the truncated section south from Selby to Doncaster consist of just two trains per day in each direction. On 1 September 1994 all four services ran during the hours of darkness, so the 'present' view was, perforce, trainless. *Both BM*

135

SELBY: In the interval of 20 years between these photographs Selby has lost its main line and major junction status. In the scene on 14 June 1974 a Manchester-bound Trans-Pennine Class 124/1 DMU stands in platform 1 with Driving Motor Composite No 51954 facing the camera. A northbound train of coal hoppers passes through double-headed with Class 37s, No 37085 leading No 37216.

Twenty years later and there is no longer any need for the centre through road, which has been lifted. The engineers' train pictured on 1 September 1994 is returning to Doncaster after maintenance work at Temple Hirst Junction and Class 56 No 56031 will shortly be running round its train. Among the minor changes the old platform 1 has now become 2. *Both BM*

SELBY: After crossing the swing-bridge over the River Ouse a southbound parcels trains takes the centre line through Selby station on 14 June 1974. Platform staff with a loaded barrow wait until Class 40 No 40155 has cleared the crossing with its train.

On 1 September 1994 Class 142 'Pacer' No 142083, adorned with sticky tape and plastic wrapping, also enters Selby across the swing-bridge. Deputising for a Class 158, the 'Pacer' is working a late-running Hull-Manchester Piccadilly service. *BM/Ken Brunt*

When the Leeds & Selby Railway reached the old riverside station at the latter point on 22 September 1834 passengers for Hull transferred to a steamer and continued their journey by way of the River Ouse, then the Humber. On 2 July 1840 the Hull & Selby Railway carried its trains across the river by means of a swing-bridge which lasted until 1891. For many years the up and down lines were gauntleted across the bridge, but this and its elevated signal box were the only abnormal features and traffic was worked just as it would be at any other crossing of the line. *BM*

SELBY: The 'past' picture typifies the East Coast Main Line as it used to be. The southbound 'Talisman' from Edinburgh Waverley to King's Cross on 22 May 1959 is recovering from the 25 mph speed restriction through Selby and pulling away round the curve under clear signals. The locomotive is Class 'A2' 'Pacific' No 60539 *Bronzino* and all around it is the paraphernalia of a mechanically worked, steam-powered railway.

Departing south from Selby on 1 September 1994, West Yorkshire PTE Class 158/9 No 158909 forms the 15.53 train from Selby to Manchester Victoria. The road bridge and lineside hut survive, but very little else! *Both BM*

Above By comparison, on the new diversion line what curves there are do not significantly inhibit speed and in this scene, captured on 1 September 1994, the 11.00 King's Cross-Glasgow Central InterCity 225 service is not planning to slow for anything except its scheduled York stop. Class 91 No 91026 is at the front end. *BM*

Below Commencing at Temple Hirst Junction (169 m 16 ch from King's Cross) the new route of the East Coast Main Line runs via links with the Leeds-Hull route (Hambleton Junctions) to Colton Junction (182 m 79 ch). In this second photograph taken on 1 September 1994 northbound Class 56 No 56081 and its tiny train of two empty steel flats has just passed the 'Leeds to Main' link at Colton Junction and is heading towards Colton North Junction. The whole of the Selby Diversion route is controlled from York panel box. *BM*

SELBY SHED: Long past top link duties on the East Coast Main Line, one of the elegant Worsdell NER 4-4-0 designs, Class 'D20/1' No 62378, stands in the shed yard at Selby (50C) on 30 August 1954. Now only the bridge remains of that scene and even the same camera angle is impossible because of garden shrubbery. *Both BM*

York

YORK: 'Welcome to York', and there is much of historic railway interest here, including in the station the famous clock. It stands above the footbridge between the main platforms, in front of the former signal box and surrounded by elaborate decorative ironwork. In the station entrance area there is a tiled map of the former North Eastern Railway system and an old NER signal brought from Haxby and re-erected on the concourse. Also included in the station complex are the imposing hotel building and William Bell's charming 1906 tea room. The nearby headquarters offices and NER war memorial complement the more modern features resulting from an expenditure of nearly £20 million on track remodelling and improved passenger facilities. *BM*

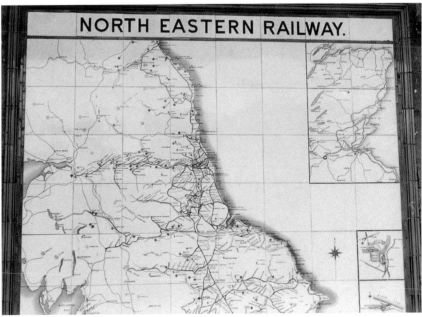

A section of the tiled wall map at York station. The former North Eastern Railway installed these unusual but useful pieces of publicity at several of its main stations. *G. Body*

YORK: The 1959 view of York shows the complex of station, hotel and former NER headquarters behind the train, and the loco depot straight ahead. The original station inside the city walls and the old museum site are off-picture to the right, while the avoiding line to the left leads to Holgate Sidings, the Carriage & Wagon Works and adjacent yards, and on to Klondyke Sidings and York Yard North signal box. Through the middle of this scene double-chimney 'A3' 'Pacific' No 60050 *Persimmon* heads south with a Newcastle- King's Cross express on 22 May.

On 28 May 1988, in the midst of alterations, Class 141 'Pacer' No 141012 departs from York with the 11.14 service to Selby. These units were constructed from Leyland National bus parts on four-wheeled underframes; after modification by Barclay this 'Pacer' was renumbered 141113.

The third photograph, taken on 1 September 1994, shows the final form of the York rationalisation. In it Class 158/9 No 158905 approaches its destination with the 10.14 from Hebden Bridge, a service that would have started from Blackpool North had this not been one of the days of the signalmen's strike. *All BM*

An exterior view of York station with its nine-arch porte-cochère and the former railway hotel beyond. *G. Body*

YORK: Under one of the four great roof spans of York station Class 'A1/1' 'Pacific' No 60113 *Great Northern* makes its scheduled stop on 29 August 1954 with a down express for Newcastle. Designed by the North Eastern Railway's architect Thomas Prosser to replace the 1841 York & North Midland station, work on the new through station at York was completed by William Peachey in 1877.

Not a great deal has changed in the 29 October 1977 view except that a 'Deltic' now heads better stock and repainting has emphasised the elegance of the rib support column spandrels. The train is the down 'Aberdonian' and the locomotive No 55006 *The Fife & Forfar Yeomanry*.

By 1 September 1994 the layout through York station has been simplified leading to the removal of the two middle roads. The cleanness of electric traction, exemplified by Class 91 91026 with the 08.00 'Scottish Pullman' from King's Cross to Glasgow, helps the whole station to appear cleaner and brighter. *All BM*

YORK: Two further views before and after remodelling at York: in the first Class 55 'Deltic' No 9009 *Alycidon* is pictured on 25 November 1973 at the head of the 08.25 up express from Newcastle to King's Cross. In the second a down service, the 09.00 King's Cross to Edinburgh, is occupying the same spot on 1 September 1994. Out of sight at the front of the train is Class 91 91020, while before the camera is Mk IV DVT No 82213, which will lead the train on its return journey. *Both BM*

YORK: In addition to its importance as a major stopping point on the East Coast Main Line, York has always had an important role as an interchange station. It has trunk cross-Pennine and North East/South West services plus local workings to Leeds (via Harrogate and via Church Fenton), Sheffield, Hull and Scarborough. The only significant closures have been the Market Weighton and Pickering lines. In the south bay platforms on 4 December 1976 stand two typical York local services. The 17.43 service to Sheffield and the 17.38 to Leeds are headed respectively by Class 101/1 'Calder Valley' DMBS No E51815 and Rolls Royce-engined Metro-Cammell 111 DMBS No 50136.

The same spot on 1 September 1994 is occupied by Class 158/0 Regional 'Express' No 158774. This working would normally have been one of the Scarborough-Blackpool North trains across the Pennines, but as this was a strike day the unit was running as the truncated 10.14 York to Hebden Bridge. *Both BM*

YORK: These views show the sharp curve to the Scarborough line top right. On 7 September 1977 Class 47 No 47426 is drawing into the station with a King's Cross relief train from Newcastle. At the opposite platform stands the first of the Eastern Region Class 254 HSTs, No 254001, which is operating on York-Darlington trials and clearly attracting interest in the process.

The train arriving at York on 1 September 1994 is the 09.21 Middlesbrough-Manchester Airport service formed of Class 158/0 No 158800. Over recent years Regional Railways have introduced a number of new services of this kind, increasing the permutation of through trains connecting important regional centres. *Both BM*

YORK: From its earliest days York has been important in motive power terms, providing locomotives for main-line services and dozens of other turns. With so many different pre-Grouping railways running trains to and from York it is hardly surprising that at one time it had as many as six engine sheds. These two views are of the interior of the surviving shed in diesel days, on 21 September 1975 and 7 September 1977 respectively. Diesel machines in the first view include Brush Class 47/4 No 47542 and Class 55 No 55010 *The King's Own Scottish Borderer*, but the centre stage is occupied by '2800' Class 2-8-0 No 2818. The locomotive has just arrived and looks in superb condition for its role as part of the National Collection at the National Railway Museum. Three Brush 47/4s pose in the second view, Nos 47432, 47460 and 47541. *Both BM*

YORK: Home of the headquarters of the proud North Eastern Railway, York has a record of caring for its railway heritage. Its first railway museum used the site of the 1841-77 station and included among its exhibits GN 4-2-2 No 1 pictured there on 22 May 1959. Patrick Stirling built the first of these 'Singles' at Doncaster in 1870. More followed and soon they were handling all the principal expresses on the main line, a task they carried out with distinction until the end of the century. No 1 was withdrawn in 1907 and spent a period stored in King's Cross shed before finding a more permanent home in the York Museum.

The National Railway Collection is now cared for by the National Railway Museum at its home in Leeman Road just west of the station. This interior view taken on 4 December 1976 includes several locomotive types that worked top trains on the East Coast Main Line, including the two 'Atlantics' (which appear among the earlier King's Cross scenes), an 'A4' and a North Eastern 4-4-0. *Both BM*

10.
THIRSK AND NORTHALLERTON

The stretch of line north from York sees the beginning of a collection of lineside signs like this one marking 200 miles to Edinburgh. *BM*

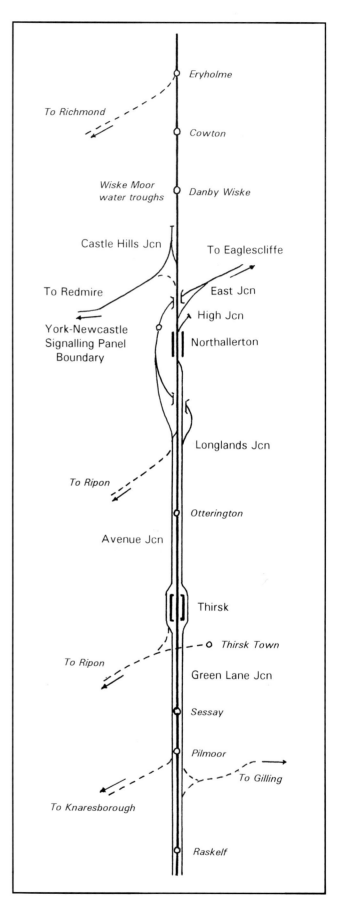

Eryholme

To Richmond

Cowton

Wiske Moor water troughs — Danby Wiske

Castle Hills Jcn — To Eaglescliffe

To Redmire — East Jcn

High Jcn

York-Newcastle Signalling Panel Boundary — Northallerton

Longlands Jcn

To Ripon

Otterington

Avenue Jcn

Thirsk

To Ripon — Thirsk Town

Green Lane Jcn

Sessay

Pilmoor

To Gilling

To Knaresborough

Raskelf

Pilmoor and Thirsk

PILMOOR: Beyond York the East Coast Main Line passes via Clifton Sidings to Skelton to rejoin the avoiding line and shed the route to Harrogate. Then comes Skelton Bridge and a crossing of the River Ouse as a prelude to a long, straight and flat entry to the Vale of York. Along this stretch lie the sites of former stations at Beningbrough, Tollerton and Alne, the latter the junction for the Easingwold Railway. 'At or near Tollerton' was the changeover point stipulated for crews working non-stop steam services using corridor tenders. On the high speed stretch through Pilmoor it is now difficult to spot the remains of the former station (closed 5 May 1958 along with its neighbour Raskelf) and its junctions with the Knaresborough and Pickering/Malton lines (the latter route via Gilling was formerly used for holiday trains between Scarborough and the North). The first picture features a block train of BRT wagons heading for the border on 13 June 1974 behind Class 45 'Peak' No 50 (later 45040) *The King's Shropshire Light Infantry*. A signal box and trailing crossover appear in the distance in this photograph, but only quadruple plain track remains in the second one, along with the up-side houses. Beneath the wires a northbound engineer's train passes Pilmoor on 31 August 1994 headed by Class 56 No 56109. *Both BM*

PILMOOR: At Pilmoor the Vale of York is still a wide, fertile plain with the Hambleton Hills and the Pennines yet to close in on the route of the railway. Through this pastoral scene a steel train heads south on 13 June 1974 hauled by Class 40 No 40109. In the background a farmer is 'leading' baled straw.

The lineside bushes have become a small forest in the sec-ond view. The farmhouse is still there but the photograph is later in the season and the nearer land has been cropped. On the main line itself the 10.00 Edinburgh-King's Cross InterCity 225 express is near maximum speed passing through Pilmoor, sweeping past much slower moving Class 47/0 No 47156, which is hauling a southbound Freightliner. *Both BM*

THIRSK: An unusual locomotive combination seen south of Thirsk on 21 May 1959. 'WD' Class 2-8-0 No 90027 pilots Blackstone-engined Class 10 shunter No 13141 at the head of a southbound mixed freight that includes high-sided coal wagons and sheeted opens with tilt bars. The shunter was presumably a part of the consist and being taken to or from works.

Crossing from Slow line to Fast, the 10.18 Middlesbrough-Manchester Airport Regional 'Express', formed of Class 158/0 No 158813, picks up speed after the Thirsk stop on 31 August 1994. The camera position is pretty well the site of the overbridge leading from the old Leeds & Thirsk Railway route through Ripon and then into a terminus nearer to and aptly known as Thirsk Town. After diversion of the Ripon line trains into the main-line station the old L&T site served as a goods depot until closure in 1966. *Both BM*

THIRSK: Class 'B16/1' 4-6-0 No 61473 passes through Thirsk on 21 May 1959 hauling a Class F fast unfitted freight service. The locomotive is one of the original Raven designs built for the North Eastern Railway in 1920. Later Gresley and Thompson rebuilds of some members of the class replaced Stephenson valve gear with Walschaerts.

By 13 June 1974, the date of the second view, the vintage water tower has gone, along with the telegraph pole and telephone equipment. On the track timber sleepers have been replaced by concrete and the train motive power has moved from the steam age to diesel. The new era representative is Brush Class 47/4 'Generator' No 47409, which is in charge of the 08.55 Aberdeen to King's Cross express.

Passing under the same bridge at Thirsk on 31 August 1994 Coal Sector-liveried Class 56 No 56109 leads a single empty steel wagon. A change of camera angle has been necessary due to undergrowth, but this has produced a good view of the bridge, which was widened to accommodate the Second World War track widening, then capped during electrification. The old NER goods building has also gone. *All BM*

THIRSK: Following the formation of the North Eastern Railway in 1854 the train services to Thirsk Town were diverted to the East Coast Main Line station via the curve and junction in the foreground of this picture. A small engine shed existed in the area between the two routes until 1930. Passing Ripon Line Junction just south of Thirsk station on 21 May 1959 is 'B1' Class 4-6-0 No 61220 with a train of single bolster wagons.

The line from Melmerby to Thirsk closed on 14 September 1959, shortly after the date of the first photograph, and by the time of the second - 13 June 1974 - only the main line remained. Passing the site of the former junction on that date is Class 25/1 Type 2 Bo-Bo No 25046 with a Newcastle-bound mixed freight.

To repeat a photograph from the same position today a veritable forest would have to be cleared! *Both BM*

THIRSK: Benefiting from the gentle down gradient from Northallerton, this Newcastle-Colchester cross-country express has built up a fair speed as its passes through Thirsk station on 21 May 1959. At the leading end 'V2' Class 2-6-2 No 60812 has caught the eye of some of the train-spotters on the down platform.

Having been converted to two islands when the main line was quadrupled, a more recent rebuilding has abandoned the platform faces giving access to the main lines. Thirsk thus now has platforms to the two Slow lines only, with fences erected to protect passengers from the high speeds achieved by present-day express services passing on the main lines. One of these, the 08.00 Glasgow Central to King's Cross, is pictured on 31 August 1994. *Both BM*

Northallerton to Croft Spa

NORTHALLERTON: The former North Eastern Railway used a lot of 4-4-0 locomotives, most of them good to look at and excellent performers. Worsdell Class 'D20' No E2372 enters Northallerton station in the summer of 1949 with stock from the sidings to form the 5.05 pm train to Leeds via Ripon. Just into the BR era, this 4-4-0 has 'British Railways' on its tender but has yet to acquire the '6' prefix in place of the 'E' in its number.

The second photograph shows just how much things have changed. The dingy traditional station has been replaced by a simple, cleaner one - albeit with less cover - and beautiful, grimy steam has given way to electrification and this Class 158/0 Regional 'Express' on its way from Middlesbrough to Manchester Airport. The date is 6 September 1994 and the unit No 158810 (although the number has peeled off the end facing the camera). *J. W. Hague (N. E. Stead collection)/BM*

NORTHALLERTON was formerly a junction of some importance, particularly with the old Leeds Northern Railway route from Leeds and extended on to Eaglescliffe and Stockton in 1852. It also had a lonely single-line route west through Wensleydale to the Midland at Hawes, used until recently for limestone traffic from Redmire to British Steel. Complicated junctions existed north and south of the station, most of them still in use. The scene in this photograph captures Brush Class 60 No 60030 *Cir Mhor* at the head of empty steel-carrying wagons from Etruria to Lackenby. The location is East Junction and the date 22 March 1991. The train has left the main line at Longlands Junction, passed west of the station via the old branch platforms, then continued beneath the ECML by the bridge just visible behind the last wagon. *BM*

ERYHOLME: From Northallerton the East Coast Main Line takes a straight, flat course to Danby Wiske, once the site of water troughs. It then rises through the former station at Cowton to the site of Eryholme Junction where the line from Richmond joined. Nothing now breaks the 14-mile fast stretch from Northallerton to Darlington as Metro-Cammell Class 156 'Sprinter' No 156443 makes the most of the route and its pastoral scenery on 30 August 1994. The 156 is deputising for a Class 158 unit that would normally work this 14.22 service from Liverpool Lime Street to Newcastle. *BM*

DALTON-ON-TEES: This evocative scene was recorded on 21 September 1975 near the old Croft Spa station and the main line's crossing of the River Tees. Recalling the delight of the LNER livery, 'The North Eastern' steam special from Sheffield to Newcastle is hauled by Class 'B1' 4-6-0 No 1306 *Mayflower* and 'A3' 'Pacific' No 4472 *Flying Scotsman*.

A view from exactly the same position is now no longer possible because of the density of the trees growing at the lineside. However, the sight of Class 91 No 91002 *Durham Cathedral* speeding north with the 13.00 King's Cross–Edinburgh train does capture the excitement of a new railway age. *Both BM*

11.
DARLINGTON
AND
DURHAM

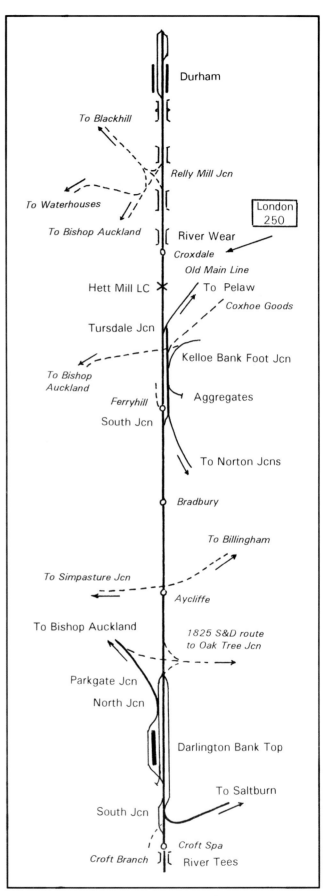

Darlington has a significant railway history dating back to its links with the 1825 Stockton & Darlington Railway. For many years the latter's 0-4-0 No 1 *Locomotion* was on display at the head of the station's London-end bays. Seen there on 13 June 1974, the locomotive has now moved to North Road station, the non-operational part of which has become the Darlington Railway Centre & Museum. *Locomotion's* place at Bank Top has been taken by a display panel depicting the S&D route and history while the station's down platform houses the great bell from the west entrance tower. *BM*

Darlington

DARLINGTON: On 13 June 1974 the 09.12 Newcastle to King's Cross departs from Darlington hauled by Class 55 'Deltic' No 55011 *Royal Northumberland Fusiliers*. Behind the train are the three great roof arches of Darlington station, supported by outer brick screen walls and by Corinthian iron columns on the central island platform. The main lines pass around the east side of the station, which dates from 1887 with a two-part restoration in the 1980s.

With Class 91 No 91005 *Royal Air Force Regiment* out of sight at the rear, the 10.00 Glasgow Central-King's Cross InterCity 225 departs from Darlington on 29 August 1994 with Mk IV DVT No 82230 leading. *Both BM*

DARLINGTON: On 28 August 1954 Class 'A8' 4-6-2T No 69859 is pulling out of Darlington Bank Top station with the 5.56 pm train to Saltburn. British locomotive designers produced very few 4-6-2T engines and this class was, in fact, a rebuild of a group of 45 4-4-4T machines. With 5 ft 9in driving wheels and the extra adhesion deriving from the rebuild they proved quite versatile performers.

Moving on to the diesel locomotive era and the trusty Class

47s, Class 47/4 No 47418 is pictured on 12 June 1974 getting away from its Darlington stop with the 17.23 Newcastle-King's Cross express.

A step further forward in time and the Saltburn service is in the hands of single Leyland Bus Class 153 diesel unit No 153319. The train is the 13.30 service from Darlington on 29 August 1994 and it will do the journey in 20 minutes less than its steam counterpart. *BM (2)/Ken Brunt*

With the erstwhile Darlington DMU maintenance depot in the background, Class 46 'Peak' No 46018 enters Darlington station with the 13.22 Newcastle-Liverpool Lime Street train on 19 March 1983. These engines, originally numbered D138-193, date from 1961 and were the final 'Peak' variant. The station lies to the left, with the entrance from the road underbridge beside the locomotive, leaving the main lines to continue ahead to its right. The footbridge from which this shot was taken has now been enclosed to make it vandal-proof, thus making a comparative view impossible. Darlington station has not changed much physically, although its appearance has been much improved by repainting. *BM*

DARLINGTON: On the up lines around the east side of Darlington station Class 'A2/3' 'Pacific' No 60512 *Steady Aim* restarts a full load on 20 May 1959 after getting a signal check. The locomotive is at the head of the 'Aberdeen Fish', a notable and important freight service run at Class C speeds so as not to delay the load of fish freshly caught by the Scottish fishing fleet. The boxes of iced herring and other fish needed to arrive at King's Cross for cartage to Billingsgate market early enough to ensure the best prices.

There is now no Aberdeen fish train nor signal to check its modern passenger counterpart. Pictured at the same spot on 29 August 1994, the 07.55 Aberdeen-King's Cross InterCity HST is led by Class 43 power car No 43119. *Both BM*

DARLINGTON SHED (51A) on 28 August 1954, and the locomotive is 'J25' Class 0-6-0 No 65688, a design originated by W. Worsdell for the North Eastern Railway back in 1898. *BM*

Having arrived on a train from Saltburn on 28 August 1954 Class 'A8' 'Pacific' tank No 69851 awaits coal and water in the shed yard before making the return journey.

Today nothing remains of the former engine shed and adjacent yards; a whole complex of running and maintenance buildings, sidings, turntable, ashpits and the like have all gone, and only the church steeple provides a location reference.

Other railway casualties in the Darlington area include Darlington locomotive works and the wagon works at Shildon, along the Bishop Auckland line. Established back in 1863, the former had undertaken all new locomotive building for the NER from 1910, but turned out its last steam locomotive in 1957. *Both BM*

DARLINGTON S&D CROSSING: The original course of the pioneer Stockton & Darlington Railway made a flat crossing of the East Coast Main Line just north of Darlington Bank Top. At one period spurs linked the intersecting routes, but a new line from Darlington South Junction to Oak Tree Junction in 1887 allowed trains from the Bishop Auckland direction to serve both Darlington stations and avoid the right-angle crossing of the main line. Thereafter only declining goods and engineers' traffic used the direct Parkgate to Oak Tree line, which eventually closed from 21 May 1967. The S&D crossing and its signal box were still there when a summer special with the headboard 'CTAC Scottish Tours Express' was photographed on 28 August 1954. The 'B1' Class engine is so dirty that its number cannot be deciphered.

All that remains of the S&D crossing today is the lineside sign, passing which is the 05.04 Bristol Temple Meads-Newcastle InterCity HST led by Class 43 power car No 43194 on 29 August 1994. *Both BM*

Durham

FERRYHILL: North of Darlington the East Coast Main Line rises via the former stations at Aycliffe and Bradbury, then descends again to Ferryhill. It is joined there by the line from Stockton to create a four-track section through the former station, which lost its passenger services on 6 March 1967. On 29 August 1994 Class 153 No 153307 is working the 13.55 train from Gateshead Metro Centre to Saltburn at the north end of the Ferryhill complex, with Thrislington Quarry in the background. From this area lines formerly radiated to Bishop Auckland, Sunderland, Hartlepool and Coxhoe, as well as the old main-line route via Leamside. *BM*

DURHAM is approached by a curving, wooded section of the route shaped by the Wear, Deerness and Browney rivers. This is followed by a high viaduct, which leads the railway round the west of the historic city and affords an impressive view of the castle and cathedral standing above a bend in the Wear. The Norman castle was the home of the Prince-Bishops of the Palatinate of Durham until 1857, which was the year that the line through Durham opened, albeit then part of the Leamside-Bishop Auckland branch. This scene was captured on 27 May 1980 with Class 37 No 37010 heading south across the viaduct with a block train load of Blue Circle cement in bulk Presflo wagons. *BM*

DURHAM: With a number of barrier wagons protecting the locomotive and crew from the load of ICI anhydrous ammonia tanks, Class 25/2 No 25203 crosses Durham Viaduct heading south on 27 May 1980. The ten-arch viaduct, which spans a tributary of the River Wear, was one of the first civil engineering works to be completed by the North Eastern Railway after its formation.

By the time of the second photograph, taken on 24 August 1994, the viaduct masonry has been cleaned giving the structure a proud appearance that was much less apparent in its previous dirty state. In the process, but less obvious, the trackbed has been waterproofed and a layer of concrete placed beneath the ballast. The train is the 16.05 local service from Newcastle to Saltburn worked by Class 142 'Skipper' No 142024. which is still in the brown and cream livery of previous West Country deployment. *Both BM*

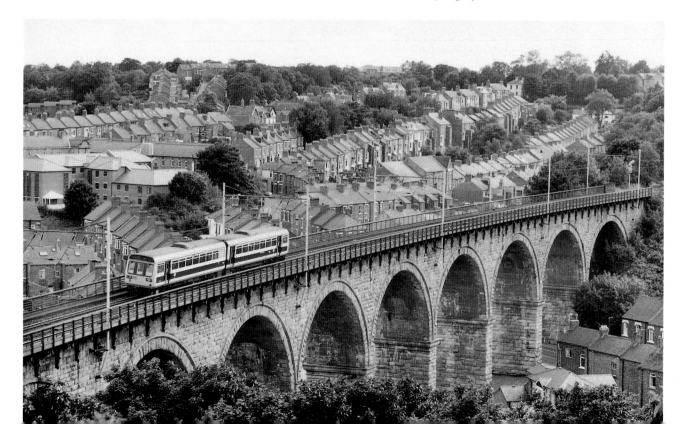

DURHAM: The Tudor-Gothic station at Durham harmonises well with its historic surroundings. Formerly it had a castellated portico, but this had gone by the time the first picture was taken. Subsequent refurbishment has added an entrance awning, attractive new chimney pots and a repaired platform canopy. Other changes at Durham include removal of up-side sidings and realignment to lift the former 30 mph speed limit. Beyond the city, at Newton Hall, another realignment lifted the previous 55 mph to 85 mph. The train in the photograph taken on 28 May 1988 is the 17.05 local service from Newcastle, which is worked by Alexander/Barclay Class 143 'Pacer' No 143020. On 29 August 1994 the unit is a Leyland Bus Class 142 'Pacer'. *Both BM*

12.
CHESTER-LE-STREET AND NEWCASTLE

To Berwick-upon-Tweed

Forth and Railway St depots

Newcastle-upon-Tyne

West Jcn

East Jcn

King Edward Bridge

River Tyne

High Level Bridge

Gateshead Loco

To Sunderland

Askew Road Tnl (53yds)

Bensham

To Carlisle

Low Fell Jcn

Low Fell

Loco.
Wagon Repairs

Tyne Yard

Lamesley

Pontop & Jarrow

Birtley

Ouston Jcn

To Tyne Dock

To Consett

Chester-le-Street

Plawsworth

Newton Hall Jcn

To Leamside

A BR successor to the 'Silver Jubilee'. . .

NEWCASTLE EXECUTIVE

NEWCASTLE
via
Darlington
Durham

K

Chester-le-Street and Tyne Yard

CHESTER-LE-STREET: From Durham the East Coast Main Line descends steadily towards the outskirts of Newcastle, passing through the former station at Plawsworth on the 2½ miles of 1 in 150 downgrade that leads to Chester-le-Street. The station there is the only one remaining open between Durham and Newcastle, but it is well served by local trains and through services to Saltburn, Leeds and Liverpool. In the first photograph a Cravens Class 105 Metro-Cammell Class 101 two-car DMU hybrid arrives at Chester-le-Street on 28 May 1980 forming the 15.25 'stopper' from Darlington to Newcastle. Driving trailer No E56460 leads DMBS No E51218.

Both foliage and trees have proliferated in the interval before the second view, which features Class 60 No 60068 *Charles Darwin* hauling northbound merry-go-round wagons through Chester-le-Street on 29 August 1994. Brush-built with Mirrlees Blackstone engines, the Class 60 locomotives first appeared in 1989 and now handle a significant proportion of the railway freight activity. *Both BM*

173

CHESTER-LE-STREET: The goods shed is all that survives of former freight activity at Chester-le-Street, which used to have a full range of yard facilities as well as private sidings for confectionery and for South Moor Colliery. However, the only freight business in evidence on 28 May 1980 was the load of cement Presflo wagons passing by behind Class 37 No 37015.

The goods shed has proved itself a survivor - now in private hands, it is passed on 29 August 1994 by the DVT-led 16.50 InterCity 225 service from Newcastle to King's Cross. *Both BM*

TYNE YARD: North of Ouston Junction the main line reverts to quadruple track as far as Low Fell Junction. Along the west side is what remains of the once great Tyne Yard, a sophisticated hump freight yard built for marshalling traffic to and from the dozens of depots and sidings on Tyneside. The view on 11 February 1979 shows Tyne Yard shed (TY) with two Class 47s, Nos 47288 and 47409, four Class 08 shunters, Nos 08325, 08445, 08671 and 08708, and Gardner-engined 03059 standing with a conflat wagon on the stops; the North East was one of the last outposts of the Class 03 machines.

Gateshead locomotive works has long gone but at least the residual wagon works activity has survived, albeit at Tyne Yard. There, in September 1994, Tyne Yard Depot was also reopened, after several years of disuse, for the maintenance of diesel locomotives. *Both BM*

TYNE YARD: The ECML section between Chester-le-Street and Newcastle formerly had stations at Birtley, Lamesley, Low Fell and Bensham, and a train service to Blackhill as well as along the main line itself. Lamesley closed in 1945 and was swallowed up by Tyne Yard, the others losing their passenger trains between 1952 and 1955. The main line here was also crossed by two historic mineral railway routes, that of the Stanhope & Tyne just north of Chester-le-Street, then the Pontop & Jarrow north of Birtley. The noted Tyne Dock-Consett iron ore trains used the former, which was linked with the main line at Ouston Junction. On the section between Lamesley and Low Fell the LNER's Class 'A4' 'Pacific' No 4464 *Bittern* is pictured just before the war with a northbound express.

After a lengthy period out of service awaiting spares, Class 91 No 91013 passes the same spot on 20 July 1994 on a northbound trial run with a short formation of Mk IV stock. The main line has been banked above what is now the goods line to Tyne Yard. Behind the foliage the field is now a housing estate, but the bridge remains as a point of reference. *W. B. Greenfield (courtesy NELPG)/Ken Groundwater*

Gateshead

GATESHEAD: From Low Fell a connection leads west to the Carlisle line, which then passes beneath the main line to join it at King Edward Bridge South Junction. This is the viewpoint in these two photographs, looking towards North Junction and the bridge itself, and with the line to East Junction and the High Level Bridge curving away to the right. Newcastle's Metro bridge across the Tyne appears in these pictures beyond the railway bridge, while on the left between the railway and river is the area of the original 1837 line from Carlisle. Class 37 No 37068 features in the photograph taken on 11 February 1979 at the head of an engineers' train that has passed over the Tyne via King Edward Bridge and is heading on to Tyne Yard.

In the second view, this time dated 29 August 1994, Class 142 'Pacer' No 142022 in Tyne & Wear PTE livery is working the 16.52 service from Nunthorpe via Middlesbrough, Sunderland and Newcastle to Carlisle. *Both BM*

GATESHEAD SHED: Before the involvement of Edinburgh Haymarket, Gateshead (52A) and King's Cross were the main providers of locos and men for the principal East Coast Main Line expresses, and Gateshead locomen made a major contribution to the express steam years, albeit with something better than the Class 'J25' veteran pictured at the shed on 26 August 1954, in use as a stationary boiler.

After closure for steam traction, Gateshead MPD was converted for the maintenance of diesel locomotives. Then, when this facility was no longer needed in the area, a number of buildings on the site continued in use for wagon repairs, still the function when this photograph was taken from the same position on 29 August 1994. The premises have now closed completely, with the wagon repair facility being transferred to Tyne Yard. *Both BM*

GATESHEAD DIESEL MAINTE-NANCE DEPOT: *Above* An overall view of the depot on 11 February 1979 shows in the foreground the line from King Edward Bridge South Junction to East Junction, then Greenfield and Park Lane Junctions, which make up the base of another triangle, south of High Level Bridge. The latter, which carries road traffic on its lower deck, is visible behind Queen Elizabeth Bridge, which itself carries Metro rapid transit trains to and from the former BR South Shields line. The top of the Tyne Bridge is also just visible above the depot building. The long footbridge from which this view was recorded has been demolished and an up-to-date shot would necessitate either a low-flying helicopter or a very long ladder! *BM*

Above right and right A damaged Class 37, three 'Peaks' and a Class 08 shunter stand outside the south end of the depot on 11 February 1979. The 08 Class represent an unglamorous, unpraised design that has done sterling work all over the rail network since its introduction in 1952. Built by BR with 350 hp English Electric engines and EE traction motors, the 08s have humped, shunted, tripped, piloted and marshalled every kind of traffic with an excellent record of performance and reliability.

Fifteen years on one will doubtless move the two wagonloads of bogies remaining at the now closed and moved Gateshead Wagon Repair Works, photographed on 29 August 1994. *Both BM*

Newcastle -upon- Tyne

NEWCASTLE-UPON-TYNE: *Top* Hauling a northbound merry-go-round coal train, Class 56 No 56118 comes off King Edward Bridge and threads its way past Newcastle West Junction on 30 August 1994. The photograph was taken from the west end of the station and the single line ahead leads to all that remains of the 1839 route to Carlisle along the north bank of the Tyne. Passenger services on this route have, over the years, switched from the Tyne's south to north bank and back again, the north bank portion being eventually curtailed to the engineers' Forth Sidings and Castle Cement terminal at Railway Street. *BM*

Above left and left Prior to remodelling of the track and signalling at Newcastle the Main plus Up and Down KEB West lines led to the platform lines and to four avoiding lines round the river side of the station. On 4 August 1978 Class 40 No 40069 is pictured on these avoiding lines with an up ballast train made up of 'Mermaid' and 'Dogfish' wagons. No 40069 is the unique member of the class with external drainage pipes and cutaway body skirt.

Newcastle now has a new pair of platforms, one beyond the former outer wall, being used here on 30 August 1994 by Class 142 'Pacers' No 142066 and No 142071 waiting to depart with the 11.15 from Sunderland to Gateshead Metro Centre. *Both BM*

NEWCASTLE-UPON-TYNE: Moving the camera a little to the left, on 4 August 1978 we see English Electric Class 40 No 40068 arriving with the 11.50 from Edinburgh. Forming, with the two Tyne bridges, part of a rail circle linking four routes and two triangles, almost any working is possible at Newcastle. However, this train is at a normal down platform and the avoiding lines are normally paired down and up from left to right.

The up-to-date scene on 30 August 1994 again shows how much has changed at Newcastle, including the two new platforms on either side of the outer wall. Class 56s Nos 56107 and 56035 are pictured travelling 'light engine' to Tyne Yard after an unbalanced working, and pass Class 156 'Sprinter' No 156443, which has arrived from Liverpool Lime Street. *Both BM*

NEWCASTLE-UPON-TYNE: Class 'A1' 'Pacific' No 60159 *Bonnie Dundee* is an apt choice to head the southbound 'Heart of Midlothian' service on 27 August 1954. The scene is typical of the period and includes some interesting features - electric lighting as well as a traditional oil lamp on the locomotive, a lovely pair of NER subsidiary signals, some unusual canopy decoration, and the quaintest of water supply apparatus.

Simplicity is the keynote of the changes revealed in the second scene. Both the centre track and the end screen of the roof have gone and the canopies have lost their frills. The date is 30 August 1994, the train a southbound parcels service and the motive power Class 47/4 No 47833, which has been returned to the original two-tone green livery and pre-TOPS number D1962. *Both BM*

NEWCASTLE-UPON-TYNE: Another view at the same platforms captures all the atmosphere of the steam age. The two Class 'V2' 2-6-2s are less clean than they might be, but these, above most other engines, were the jacks of all trades and ranked high in the utilisation statistics. Admired by young spotters, No 60847 *St Peter's School York AD 627*, a York-based engine, is nearest the camera and has brought in a train from Liverpool Lime Street on 27 August 1954.

Along with the handbarrows, both staff and spotters have gone in the 30 August 1994 view. The train is the 12.03 HST to Birmingham New Street headed by Class 43 power car No 43153 *University of Durham. Both BM*

NEWCASTLE-UPON-TYNE: A classic pre-war shot of the first and most famous 'A4' streamlined 'Pacific', No 2509 *Silver Link*, at Newcastle in 1938, heading the northbound 'Coronation' on its way to Edinburgh Waverley. Topping up with water and blowing off steam in every direction, the impressive locomotive shows signs of patchwork in the valances, which were subsequently removed to improve access to the motion.

The difference between the profile of the 'A4' and that of Class 91 No 91023 is not all that great considering that one derived from a model and wind tunnel and the other from sophisticated aerodynamic studies. The Class 91 heads the 07.30 service from King's Cross on 24 October 1994. Recent changes to the surrounding station area include reprofiling the platform with a 45-yard extension and a 9 cm increase in height to conform to EEC regulations. *W. B. Greenfield (courtesy NELPG)/Ken Groundwater*

NEWCASTLE-UPON-TYNE: The bays at the west end of Newcastle station have traditionally been used, since the end of the electric services, for loading parcels traffic and for trains originating here for the Carlisle line. Seen in the first photograph, which was taken on 4 August 1978, Metro-Cammell Class 101/2 DMU No E51216 is taking on passengers for its 12.40 service to Carlisle. On the left stand Class 3 shunters Nos 03056 and 03170, together with a collection of parcels vans.

On 30 August 1994 Class 47/4 No D1962 (47833) *Captain Peter Manisty RN* prepares to leave Newcastle with a southbound Res parcels working. The rationalisation changes again show in the new canopies, truncated platform and reduction from four running lines to two. *Both BM*

NEWCASTLE-UPON-TYNE: A well-known landmark at the eastern end of Newcastle station is the castle keep built in 1172 on the site of the 'new castle'. Its 'nomme de guerre', Bridle of the Scots, was a reference to its front-line role in restraining cross-border incursions from the north. Following a naming ceremony at Newcastle station on 5 December 1992 Class 91 No 91009 *Saint Nicholas* departs on the 11.30 service to King's Cross. The train was routed via the High Level Bridge in order to place the locomotive in its usual running position at the rear. Note the speed restrictions resulting from the tight curves. *BM*

Like King's Cross, Peterborough, Doncaster and York, Newcastle has been the subject of a complete track and signalling rationalisation scheme. The sweeping extent of the changes is apparent in these high-level views from the castle. The total amount of track has been cut by well over half, reducing wear on awkward points and sharp curves and lessening conflicting movements. In the process there has also been a considerable gain in car parking space.

The east end view on 29 May 1980 shows no fewer than seven trains including two HSTs, three Cravens Class 105 DMUs and a Metro-Cammell Class 101. The South Shields service in the foreground had taken over from the old NER electric trains and has now gone underground through Central station as part of the Metro system.

On 30 August 1994 the foreground train in the revised layout is the 10.04 Gateshead Metro Centre-Sunderland formed of Class 142 'Pacers' Nos 142066/071. *Both BM*

NEWCASTLE station was built in 1850 for the York, Newcastle & Berwick Railway with three Arch with John Dobson as the architect and Robert Stephenson as engineer. Later the original three spans grew to five, the platforms to 15 and a portico was added. Like York it offers much to the interested observer, from the classical frontage and adjoining hotel to the ultra-modern travel centre on the concourse. In this second pair of 'aerial' views, looking back a few years earlier to 29 May 1980, Class 55 'Deltic' No 55002 *The*

King's Own Yorkshire Light Infantry is involved in one of the many former unavoidable conflicting movements as it heads northbound from Newcastle and over the noted diamond crossings with the 05.50 King's Cross-Aberdeen.

On 30 August 1994 the 09.49 Newcastle-Morpeth train, formed of Class 142 'Pacer' No 142018, sets out on its journey across the much rationalised layout. *Both BM*

189

NEWCASTLE-UPON-TYNE: Crossing Newcastle High Level Bridge on 29 May 1980 Metro-Cammell Class 101 twins form the 11.12 service from Sunderland to Newcastle and the 11.35 from Newcastle to Sunderland. Robert Stephenson's six-span, two-tier bridge was built in 1849 and opened by Queen Victoria. A year later there were further celebrations to mark the opening of the station and the completion of the Royal Border Bridge at Berwick, thus providing a stable through rail route to Edinburgh via what became known as the East Coast Main Line, a fitting note on which to end our 268-mile journey from King's Cross. *BM*

APPENDIX

Table of distances
between principal stations, junctions and tunnels

	M	Ch		M	Ch
King's Cross	00	00	Newark Crossing	120	63
Gasworks Tunnel		22	Askham Tunnel	134	37
Copenhagen Tunnel		65	Retford	138	49
Finsbury Park	2	41	Loversall Carr Junction	152	00
Harringay West Junction	3	29	Black Carr Junction	153	18
Wood Green Junction (Down)	4	68	Potteric Carr Junction	154	02
Alexandra Park	4	78	Balby Bridge Tunnel	155	34
Wood Green Junction (Up)	5	07	Bridge Junction	155	38
Wood Green Tunnel	5	41	South Yorkshire Junction	155	58
Barnet Tunnel	7	42	Doncaster	156	77
New Barnet	9	12	Marshgate Junction	156	28
Hadley Wood South Tunnel	10	21	Shaftholme Junction	160	16
Hadley Wood North Tunnel	10	60	Joan Croft Junction	160	48
Potters Bar Tunnel	11	25	Temple Hirst Junction	169	16
Potters Bar	12	57	Hambleton South Junction	174	10
Hatfield	17	54	Hambleton North Junction	174	75
Welwyn Garden City	20	25	Colton Junction	182	79
Welwyn South Tunnel	22	11	Colton North Junction	183	65
Welwyn North Tunnel	22	44	Holgate Junction	188	08
Langley Junction (Up)	26	45	York	188	40
Langley Junction (Down)	26	61	Skelton	190	11
Stevenage	27	45	Thirsk	210	56
Hitchin	31	74	Longlands Junction	217	31
Cambridge Junction	32	11	Northallerton	218	36
Biggleswade	41	13	High Junction	218	49
Sandy	44	10	Castle Hills Junction	219	23
St Neots	51	58	Darlington South Junction	232	21
Huntingdon	58	70	Darlington	232	50
Fletton Junction	75	02	Parkgate Junction	233	18
Crescent Junction	76	25	Ferryhill South Junction	244	57
Peterborough	76	29	Tursdale Junction	247	31
Werrington Junction	79	34	Durham	254	53
Stoke Tunnel	100	39	Chester-le-Street	260	32
Grantham	105	38	Low Fell Junction	265	77
Nottingham Branch Junction	106	08	Askew Road Tunnel	267	66
Peascliffe Tunnel	107	65	King Edward Bridge South Junction	268	02
Barkston South Junction	109	56	King Edward Bridge North Junction	268	17
Newark Northgate	120	08	Newcastle	268	56
Newark Crossing South Junction	120	48			

INDEX

'A1-A3' Class locomotives 11, 13, 28, 31, 35, 46, 59, 73, 77, 89, 99, 101-102, 116, 132, 138, 143, 145, 161, 166, 182

'A4' Class locomotives 2, 12-15, 19, 22, 24, 38, 44, 50, 56, 60-61, 75, 84, 98-99, 118, 135, 176, 185

Abbots Ripton 92

Alexandra Palace, see Wood Green

Arlesey 81

Askham 118

Barkston 110

Belle Isle, King's Cross 27-28

Biggleswade 82-83

Bounds Green 48-49

Brickyards 94

Bridges 9, 29, 43, 71, 115, 137, 153, 169-170, 179-180

Chester-le-Street 173-174

Coal traffic 71, 78, 86, 100, 136, 173, 180

Conington 93

Corby Glen 106

'Coronation' service 12, 22, 185

Crow Park 116

Dalton-on-Tees 161

Darlington 163-168
  shed 167

'Deltic' locomotives 14-15, 20-21, 40, 55, 69, 77, 119, 145, 147, 150, 163, 189

Diesel multiple units 39, 64, 67, 83, 87, 91, 109, 112, 129, 136, 148, 173, 186-187, 190

Doncaster station 127-130
  Bridge Junction 123
  Marshgate Junction 131
  shed 126
  Works 132-133
  yard 124-125

Durham 169-171

Engineering department 79, 81-82, 119, 125, 136, 153, 177, 180

Eryholme 160

Essendine 10, 101-102

Ferme Park 43

Ferryhill 169

Finsbury Park 37-40

Flat crossings 115, 120, 168

'Flying Scotsman' service 11-14, 105, 121

Freightliners 15, 26, 154

Ganwick 62-63

Gateshead 177
  Diesel Maintenance Depot 179
  shed 11, 178

Goods traffic 20, 40, 43, 52-53, 60, 63-64, 72, 75-76, 81-82, 84, 93, 97, 99, 107, 118, 120, 129, 131, 154-157, 160, 166, 169-170, 174

Grantham 108-110

Gresley, Sir Nigel 11-12, 23, 25, 28

Hadley Wood 59-61

Harringay 41

Hatfield 67-69

Helpston 97, 99

Hertford Loop 47

Highdyke 107

Hitchin 81

Holloway Bank 2, 14, 29-36

Holme 93

Hornsey 44
  shed 45

Hotels 20, 98, 189

Huntingdon 89-91

Journey times 9-12

King's Cross station 4, 19-23
  goods depot 26
  shed 24-25

Knebworth 77

Langley Junction 78-79

Little Bytham 105

LNER Five Year Plan 20

Locomotive sheds 24-25, 45, 99, 126, 150, 157, 167, 178

Locomotive works 132-133, 167, 175

Maintenance depots 45, 47

Marshalling yards 43, 93, 175

National Railway Museum 150-151

Nene Valley Railway 95

New Barnet 56-57

New England 99

Newark 111-113, 115

Newcastle-upon-Tyne 180-190

Northallerton 159-160

Oakleigh Park 52-55

Offord 87

Palace Gates 48

Peterborough 8, 14, 96-99
  New England shed 99

Pilmoor 153-154

Potters Bar 63-65

Retford 119-121

Sandy 84-87

Selby 135-138
  shed 140

Selby Diversion 139

'Silver Jubilee' service 12, 16, 19, 56, 60

Speed records 12, 15-16, 104, 110

Stevenage 80

Stockton & Darlington Railway 9, 162

Stoke Tunnel 106-107

Tallington 100

Thirsk 155-158

Tunnels 16, 23, 27-28, 50-51, 59-62, 64, 73, 106-107, 118

Tuxford 117

Tyne Yard 175-176

'V2' Class locomotives 23, 62-63, 71, 92, 123, 158, 183

Welham Green 66

Welwyn Garden City 70-71

Welwyn North 72

Welwyn Tunnels 73-75

'West Riding Limited' service 12, 22, 61

Wood Green 46-47
  Tunnels 50-51

Yaxley & Farcet 94

York 141-151
  railway museums 151